Thomas Fitzpatrick
and
The Lepracaun Cartoon Monthly
1905 - 1915

PORTLAND
PUBLIC LIBRARY

ENRICHING OUR COMMUNITY,
EXPANDING OUR WORLD.

GIVEN TO THE
PORTLAND PUBLIC LIBRARY
BY THE
JAMES A. HEALY FUND

Lepracaun 2015
by Conánn FitzPatrick,
Lecturer in Computer
Animation,
Ulster University

Thomas Fitzpatrick

and *The Lepracaun Cartoon Monthly*

1905-1915

1905-1915

James Curry and Ciarán Wallace

Dublin
Dublin City Council
2015

Series editors: Mary Clark & Máire Kennedy

First published 2015 by
Dublin City Council
c/o Dublin City Library and Archive
138-144 Pearse Street
Dublin 2

Comhairle Cathrach
Bhaile Átha Cliath
Dublin City Council

Decade of Commemorations

www.dublincommemorates.ie

Text © the contributors 2015
Concept © Dublin City Public Libraries and Archives
Designed by: Yellowstone Communications Design
Printed by: PrintRun

ISBN – 9781907002175

Distributed by
Four Courts Press
Malpas Street
Dublin 7
www.fourcourtspress.ie

Contents

Foreword by Jim FitzPatrick   vii

Thomas Fitzpatrick (1860-1912) by James Curry   2

The Lepracaun Cartoon Monthly by Ciarán Wallace   21

Commentaries by Ciarán Wallace

    Society   33

    City Politics   89

    National Politics   109

    Women   165

    Labour   183

Acknowledgements

All images used in this publication are copyright Dublin City Library & Archive, unless otherwise stated. The library holds a collection of 48 original cartoons on card by Thomas Fitzpatrick and a full run of *The Lepracaun Cartoon Monthly* from 1905 to 1915.

The Foreword was contributed by Jim FitzPatrick, grandson of Thomas Fitzpatrick (see: http://www.jimfitzpatrick.com/). The frontispiece, based on the cover of *The Lepracaun Cartoon Monthly*, is by Conánn FitzPatrick, Jim's son, and great-grandson of Thomas.

Special thanks are due to Mary Broderick, Prints and Drawings, National Library of Ireland for her assistance. We are grateful to Felix Larkin who offered helpful advice, to Robert Opie who provided the Sunlight Soap advertisement on p. 132, and to the late Shane MacThomáis for his assistance in connection with the Thomas Fitzpatrick family grave at Glasnevin Cemetery.

Thanks to Anne Wallace for her helpful suggestions on the commentaries and to Patrick Maume for help in identifying the caricatures of some less prominent figures. Special thanks to Ann Curry and Sandra Hartwieg for their support and encouragement.

Disclaimer

Foreword by Jim FitzPatrick

The weird and the wonderful.

Something beautiful and extraordinary happened when I recently attended a meeting at the Dublin City Library and Archive for a discussion regarding my foreword to this new book on the *Lepracaun Cartoon Monthly* and my grandfather Thomas FitzPatrick, the largely forgotten, once controversial, Irish political cartoonist and publisher, who died in 1912. You know when the hair stands up on the back of your neck? This happened to me twice that afternoon. Firstly, when historian James Curry and librarian Máire Kennedy showed me a recently acquired original Thomas FitzPatrick illuminated address.

Why was I so affected? Because it looked like my own work, both in terms of composition and execution! I had never been aware such a beautiful piece existed and I studied it intensely. I felt that strange sense of familiarity that comes occasionally from a heightened state of awareness, usually induced by strange herbal substances except I was stone cold sober and clean as a whistle.

Then, almost immediately, another psychic kick in the head when we were leafing through some later issues of the *Lepracaun* from 1912, less than a year after my grandfather's death. James held up this single poorly reproduced full page black and white rather fuzzy litho image advertising the work of Thomas FitzPatrick's daughter, Mary FitzPatrick, then a young woman of 22.

Advertisement for Mary FitzPatrick's illumination business
The Lepracaun
(Oct. 1912), p. 64.

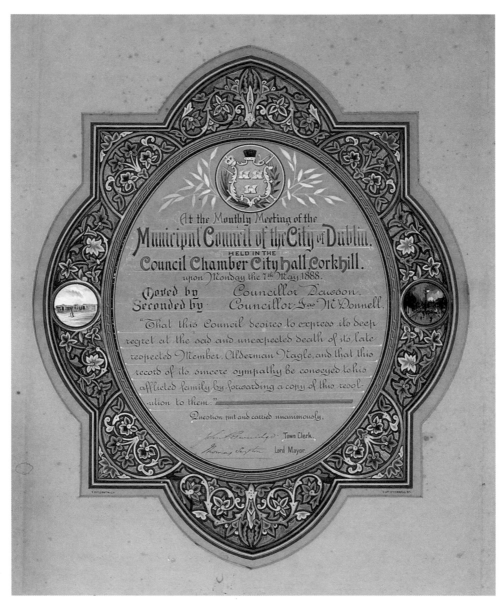

Thomas Fitzpatrick,
Illuminated address, 1888.

I was stunned once more. It was a moment of absolute revelation with a touch of déjà vu tossed in for good measure. It was a beautiful piece of what we now term 'Celtic Renaissance' artwork. I felt like I knew the artist and I most certainly knew the artwork even though I had never seen it, or anything much like it, in my own lifetime. It was produced almost over 100 years ago and I'm not that old, yet. It had so many elements of what I thought of as my own original take on Celtic Art that I was more than impressed, I was taken aback somewhat; I recognized that even though the work was so similar to my own, not just taken from elements of ancient Irish manuscripts. It was new and original, more like the later art work by Art O'Murnaghan for his epic 'Leabhar na hAiseirghe' but was also a new and interesting version of the filigree and knotwork we are so familiar with in Ireland.

When I decided back around 1970 to create the Celtic artworks I am so well known for today, I was totally unaware of this connection with my own past. What we have here between myself, Thomas FitzPatrick and his wonderfully talented daughter Mary was what Jung has described as the connection with the 'racial subconscious'.

Despite thinking that I knew quite a lot about him, I have recently grown to accept that I actually knew very little about Thomas FitzPatrick beyond the fact that he was a well-regarded, gregarious and humorous fellow who did some stunning cartoons and very passionate anti-establishment writing. My gran had often told me that 'the notorious scribbler of dirty books, James Joyce' did some 'nixers' for the publication, including the famous 'Dear, dirty Dublin' full pager (see p.95 below) and that the *Lepracaun* was one of only two publications Joyce subscribed to while in exile in Trieste.

I inherited two volumes of this publication from my mom and two of his framed illuminations some time ago when my last aunt died - and I was aware he had an 'illuminated address' business with his daughter, Mary FitzPatrick, at 6 O'Connell Street, then a beautiful streetscape lined with those magnificent plane trees and the wonderfully elegant `Nelson's Pillar'.

My father unfortunately left my mother destitute when I was aged five so I never had any proper connection with the family of my grandfather – only snippets of his life were passed to me by my mother and her mother's sister, my grand-aunt (who we all called 'Granny' Brady) who we lived with on and off for many years, in the 1950s, at 6 Saint Michael's Road in Glasnevin, after all my father's houses had been sold to pay his debts and my grandfather's studio and artwork sold off and dispersed while my 98 year old grandmother had to leave Ireland to live with her daughter Nora.

The two illuminated works handed down to me a few years ago upon the death of my aunt are religious works with beautiful but fairly typical Victorian borders but what really struck me was the proportion of border to image. I was startled to discover I had worked in much the same proportion quite unconsciously for over twenty-five years when producing a large volume of work which I loosely described as 'Celtic Art'.

Once more the Jungian 'racial subconscious' reared its befuddled head and had me scratching my own in puzzlement; is this life just a repeat of previous lives or are we directed by the unknown forces of the fast-flowing genetic stream implanted like my own rangy leggy body topped with red hair inherited from both sides of my family? Is art inherited genetically or via inherited memory perhaps? I wish I knew the answer to that one.

My son, Conánn FitzPatrick, carries on the family tradition to this day. An alumnus of Sullivan Bluth and Steven Spielberg's Dreamworks in Los Angeles, today Conánn is a lecturer in art, animation and design in Belfast College of Art, passing his skills to a whole new generation. Conánn is also responsible for the frontispiece to this volume, the computer coloured version of the original *Lepracaun* cover.

Thanks to James Curry and Ciarán Wallace I am now more aware then ever of my own debt genetically and artistically to Thomas FitzPatrick and his daughter Mary and now, more than ever I stand proud beside them hoping one day their beautiful work will once more see the light of day. For myself, that is the dream. I hope this book can act as a new beginning for the *Lepracaun* and the work of Thomas FitzPatrick and hopefully bring it to a large and appreciative new audience.

Back to the future: Today we have the various scandals, the Irish Water fiasco and a myriad of instances of cronyism exposed. It now seems that the main political parties have all had their snouts in the trough despite fervent denials at the time. All this has been verified by the various tribunals who described political corruption in Dublin and by extension the rest of the country as 'endemic'. Nothing new then, but where, oh where is Thomas FitzPatrick, the scourge of the Irish political cartel, when we need him?

JIM FITZPATRICK, 14 JANUARY 2015.

Thomas Fitzpatrick (1860-1912), by James Curry

Early Years

Thomas Fitzpatrick was born in Cork City on 27 March 1860, the son of draper William and his wife Mary.[1] He would go on to become one of the leading Irish political cartoonists of the late nineteenth and early twentieth centuries, having at an early age shown clear signs of the artistic talent that would one day 'raise him to a high place in the estimation of his countrymen'.[2] It is likely that he was the Thomas Fitzpatrick recorded as winning a prize at the Cork School of Art in 1872.[3] As a schoolboy 'Fitz' was forever drawing caricatures of his classmates, although after venturing 'to portray the master' on one occasion, it was said that this met with 'such unpleasant result' that he did not dare repeat the experiment! After leaving school, the young artist commenced an apprenticeship with the established Messrs. Guy and Company colour-printers and letterpress publishing firm at 26 Academy Street, Cork. Although Fitzpatrick would recall this period as 'seven long, weary years', the apprenticeship equipped him with an accomplished foundation of artistic skills that served him well in subsequent life.[4]

Upon the expiration of his apprenticeship Fitzpatrick relocated to Dublin, the city where he would live, with the exception of a spell spent in London during the 1880s, for the remainder of his life. He was soon employed by some of the principal Dublin printing firms, including City Printing Co. and Messrs. Hugh and Michael Woods, the latter a 'wholesale stationers, lithographic and letterpress printers and engravers' operating out of 38-43 High Street.[5] It was later said of Fitzpatrick that his labours for these firms 'did much to bring lithographic work, then in a comparatively poor state, to the level of a fine art',[6] and he would be professionally listed from 1888 until his death as a 'litho., and illuminating artist'. In 1888-89 his office was based at 5 Upper Sackville Street, and from 1890 onwards at 6 Upper Sackville Street.[7] The brief description of Fitzpatrick's primary occupation obscures the remarkable versatility of his artistic talent, for he additionally excelled at oil, watercolour

---

1   Fitzpatrick's date of birth was first established in Walter Strickland's *A Dictionary of Irish Artists* (Dublin & London, 1913), Vol. 1, pp 352-353. On 17 July 1912, when registering her father's death, Fitzpatrick's second daughter Elizabeth supplied the information that he had been 'about 52 years' old. In the July 1912 obituary piece for *The Lepracaun Cartoon Monthly* Fitzpatrick was described as born 'a little over half-a-century ago'. Mainstream newspaper obituaries at the time were equally vague about his exact birth date.
2   *Sunday Independent*, 21 July 1912.
3   Theo Snoddy, *Dictionary of Irish Artists. 20th Century* (Dublin, 2002 edition), p. 160.
4   Ibid.
5   Ibid.
6   *Sunday Independent*, 21 July 1912.
7   *Thom's Official Directory*, 1888-1912.

and miniature painting, clay modelling and photo engraving.[8] He was also an excellent cartoonist, and it would be in this field that he was destined to achieve his greatest distinction as an artist.

Establishment as a cartoonist and family life

In 1881 Fitzpatrick began contributing cartoons to *Pat*, a resuscitated Dublin weekly periodical describing itself as 'artistic, literary, humourous, satirical', that had formerly run from December 1879 to September 1880. These cartoons would be drawn under the tutelage of *Pat's* chief artist John Fergus O'Hea (c.1838-1922), a fellow Corkman who had earlier risen to prominence drawing cartoons for short-lived comic titles such as *Zozimus* (1870-72), *Ireland's Eye* (1874-75) and *Zoz* (1876-79).[9] Together the pair made *Pat,* a pro-Home Rule publication characterized by 'light verse and heavy-handed humour', a 'stimulating weekly until its collapse for financial reasons in March 1883'.[10] Shortly afterwards Fitzpatrick moved to London in the hope of improving his career and fortune, though soon 'grew tired of life in the great metropolis and returned to the Irish capital'.[11] The death of his father may have acted as an impetus. Fitzpatrick's widowed mother moved to Dublin and was living in Our Lady's Hospice at 4 Bessborough Parade when she passed away on 23 May 1890 from consumption.[12] Upon returning to Ireland Fitzpatrick took up residence at 39 Mount Pleasant Avenue, Dublin , where he was living at the time of his marriage to Mary O'Brien on 31 January 1887 at the nearby St. Nicholas Chapel.[13] The couple would have seven children together during the opening fifteen years of their marriage,

GREAT IRISH ARTIST

The late Mr. John Fergus O'Hea, the distinguished Irish artist whose death is announced

Photograph of John Fergus O'Hea, obituary, *Freeman's Journal* (6 Sept. 1922), p. 3.

Advertisement for Fitzpatrick's business from the UCD periodical *St. Stephen's (Dec. 1901).*

---

8   *Lepracaun Cartoon Monthly*, July 1912.

9   See B. P. Bowen, 'Dublin Humorous Periodicals of the 19th Century', in *Dublin Historical Review*, Vol. 13, No. 1 (March-May, 1952), pp 7-9; Elizabeth Tilly, 'Irish Political Cartoons and the New Journalism', in Karen Steele & Michael de Nie (eds.), *Ireland and the New Journalism* (New York, 2014), pp 81-98.

10   L. Perry Curtis Jr., *Apes and Angels. The Irishman in Victorian Caricature* (Washington, 1997 edition), p. 72.

11   *Lepracaun*, July 1912.

12   Mary Fitzpatrick death certificate (General Register Office).

13   Thomas Fitzpatrick and Mary O'Brien marriage certificate (General Register Office).

although the first son, William Joseph, died from 'convulsions' on 22 September 1889, aged just six months.[14] In descending order of birth, the other Fitzpatrick children were Mary, Elizabeth, Norah, Thomas, William and James.

Cartoons for late nineteenth-century nationalist newspapers

Following his marriage Fitzpatrick contributed cartoons to early issues of *Union*, although soon found himself replaced on the paper's staff by Richard Moynan, a cartoonist with far more 'genuine unionist sympathies'.[15] In 1891 he found a more natural place of employment when he was appointed as the chief cartoonist for the *National Press*, contributing a weekly colour supplement cartoon for its weekend issue that was printed by chomolithography, a time-consuming yet visually rewarding artistic method.[16] The *National Press* had been launched in May that year as an anti-Parnellite organ during the bitter split in the Home Rule movement over Charles Stewart Parnell's leadership. As a result, Fitzpatrick's main target was the 'Uncrowned King of Ireland'. For steadfastly refusing to resign over his involvement in the Katherine and William O'Shea divorce scandal, in a series of accusatory cartoons Parnell found himself villified as a selfishly destructive 'dishonoured leader'.[17] Fitzpatrick also contributed similar weekly supplement cartoons at this time to *Nation* (under the pseudonym 'Spot'), including 'The Uplifting of the Banner' on 21 February 1891. This effort saw Parnell, wearing a 'self-conceit' sash and threateningly wielding a 'manifesto' sword (that referenced his public appeal four months earlier for the Irish Parliamentary Party to stay independent of all British parties) attacked for bringing shame, discord and ruin on his country. Trampling over religion and morality, Parnell was depicted as nothing more than a 'wrecker'.[18] Family tradition maintains that these cartoons were more likely a reflection of the editorial stance of the newspapers they appeared in rather than Fitzpatrick's own personal views.[19]

Fitzpatrick continued to draw weekly supplement cartoons for the *National Press* for a number of years after its merger with the *Weekly Freeman* in early 1892, taking over from his vacating former mentor O'Hea, who stayed loyal to Parnell. It was later said that the excellence of Fitzpatrick's cartoons during this period 'evoked the heartiest praise from critics of the highest standard',[20] and

---

14 William Joseph Fitzpatrick death certificate (General Register Office).
15 See http://irishcomics.wikia.com/wiki/Thomas_Fitzpatrick_%281860-1912%29 [accessed 1 May 2014].
16 Ibid.
17 See http://irishcomics.wikia.com/wiki/Thomas_Fitzpatrick_%281860-1912%29 [accessed 1 May 2014].
18 Ibid.
19 Jim Fitzpatrick interview with author (11 May 2014).
20 *Evening Herald*, 16 July 1912.

indeed actually proved to be 'quite a feature of the political controversies' of the time.[21] It was these cartoons for the *National Press and Weekly Freeman* that were central to Fitzpatrick earning his reputation as a political cartoonist of the highest order in the mould of O'Hea.[22] One notable contribution was 'Tyrant and Toady' on 17 September 1892, which saw a rack-renting landlord and dandified John Redmond attacked for their respective roles in causing a romantically depicted tenant farmer to be unfairly evicted from his home.[23]

Weekly Freeman
(17 Sept. 1892).

Over the coming years many other cartoons also saw Fitzpatrick go about reversing some of the harsh stereotypes of the earlier anti-Fenian British comic weeklies, through a series of illustrations which 'mocked the simian Irish caricatures of British imaginations and gave graphic legitimacy to Irish nationalists' grievances and aspirations'.[24] A memorable example was 'The Frankenstein of Hatfield and His Handiwork' on 6 May 1893, which proved that Fitzpatrick 'could draw as prognathous a villain as the best English cartoonist when he wished to do so'.[25] This cartoon depicted Lord Salisbury, the leader of the Conservative Party, as Mary Shelley's popular literary sensation Victor Frankenstein, fiercely ordering his grotesque monster of 'Bigotry' to resume the fomenting of sectarian tensions in Belfast and other Irish cities in order to undermine the Irish Parliamentary

Weekly Freeman
(6 May 1893).

Weekly Freeman
(17 Aug. 1895).

21 *Irish Times*, 17 July 1912.
22 Strickland, *A Dictionary of Irish Artists*, p. 352. For more on O'Hea see http://irishcomics.wikia.com/wiki/John_Fergus_O'Hea_(c._1838-1922) [accessed 2 May 2014]. A selection of twenty-nine colour supplement cartoons by O'Hea for the *Weekly Freeman*, ranging from July 1881 to September 1890, are attractively reproduced with brief commentaries in L. Perry Curtis Jr., *Images of Erin in the Age of Parnell* (Dublin, 2000). This booklet also includes an 1892 cartoon by Fitzpatrick, and 1884/1890 cartoons by John D. Reigh, another leading Irish Home Rule cartoonist of the late nineteenth century.
23 See Curtis, *Apes and Angels*, pp 78-79.
24 Roy Douglas, Liam Harte & Jim O'Hara (eds.), *Drawing Conclusions. A cartoon history of Anglo-Irish relations, 1798-1998* (Belfast, 1998), p. 3.
25 Curtis, *Apes and Angels*, p. 79.

Party and their efforts to secure Home Rule. Fitzpatrick was here mimicking and reversing the famous anti-Fenian 'Irish Frankenstein' cartoon in the *Tomahawk* by Matt Morgan over twenty years earlier.[26]

As the nineteenth century drew to a close Fitzpatrick continued to contribute cartoons to the *Weekly Freeman and National Press*. On 26 October 1895 came his 'Brimstone and Treacle, or Killing with Kindness'. In the July general election held three months earlier the Conservatives had ousted William E. Gladstone's Liberal Party to usher in a decade of Tory rule, as Home Rule 'sank to the bottom of the British political agenda, and the new government sought to remove it completely by reviving its policy of constructive unionism'.[27] Between 1895 and 1900 this saw Gerald Balfour, the Irish Chief Secretary, administer a series of corrective socio-economic measures for Ireland as his government went about 'killing home rule with kindness'. In Fitzpatrick's cartoon an agitated Balfour tries in vain to force a smiling and scornful 'Pat' to swallow some new Tory medicine. Clutching a shillelagh, the imposing Irishman knowingly recognizes Balfour's medicine as nothing more than 'a brimstone mixture sweetened with treacle to make it more palatable'. Fitzpatrick was thus illustrating Ireland's determination to refuse abandoning her demand for self-government, and recognition that the Tory's ulterior motive was 'to undermine support for nationalists' home rule demands and defuse the perennial land problem'.[28]

There were also nationalist cartoons by Fitzpatrick relating to the centenary of the 1798 rebellion. The summer of 1897 saw Queen Victoria's diamond jubilee celebrations lead to an enormous outpouring of jingoism across Britain and parts of the British Empire, including Ireland. Resentful of this, at the time some advanced Irish nationalists organised anti-jubilee demonstrations in protest at Britain's refusal to grant Ireland independence. In 'Who Fears to Speak of '98, published on 26 June 1897, Fitzpatrick captured this 'mood of nationalist dissent'. A mournful figure of *Erin* was depicted as refusing a pitchfork-holding Brittania's call for her to join in the celebrations, instead loyally tending to the graves of the United Irishmen leaders who had died fighting for Irish freedom a century earlier. Fitzpatrick's glorifying of the failed 1798 rebellion against British rule continued in 'United Irishmen Still' on 8 January 1898. This cartoon optimistically implied that Irishmen at home and abroad were united under the 1798 flag of 'nationalist idealism', heralding a bright new dawn for the country which capitalised on a widespread upsurge in Irish patriotic feeling.[29]

---

26 Ibid., pp 79-81.
27 Douglas, Harte & O'Hara, *Drawing Conclusions*, p. 131.
28 Ibid.
29 Ibid., pp 132-133.

Throughout the late nineteenth and early twentieth century Fitzpatrick also contributed cartoons to publications such as the *Irish People*, *Irish Emerald* and *Irish Figaro*, the latter 'a breezy one penny weekly edited by Sydney Brooks, one of Dublin's leading literary gadflies'.[30] By early 1901 he and his family had moved into 10 Cabra Road in Glasnevin. The national census that year listed Fitzpatrick living at this address with his thirty-five year old housekeeper wife Mary, their five surviving children, and an eighteen year old male relative employed as a photo engraver.[31] A decade later, in the 1911 census, Fitzpatrick's wife, who had since given birth to their youngest son James, left the space for her occupation blank. This was because her household duties had now been taken over by a twenty year old Dublin 'domestic servant girl' named Dorah Adderley. Like the entire Fitzpatrick family, she was Roman Catholic in her faith.[32] One other sign of improved living conditions was the fact that the house had developed from a seven room 'second class' into a ten room 'first class' private dwelling.[33]

First issue of *The Lepracaun* (May 1905).

The Lepracaun Cartoon Monthly

The launch of *The Lepracaun Cartoon Monthly* in May 1905 saw Fitzpatrick realise a 'cherished ambition'.[34] Packed with humourous illustrations, puns, anecdotes and satirical features, the *Lepracaun* earned a level of popularity 'rarely, if ever, won by a publication of the kind in Ireland', running for almost ten years.[35] The name of the journal is spelled differently to the modern conventional 'leprechaun', although the contemporaneous existence of 'Lepracaun Cigarettes'

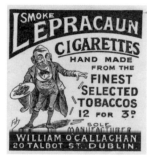

Advertisement for Lepracaun Cigarettes *The Lepracaun* (Dec. 1907), p.147.

30 Curtis, *Apes and Angels*, p. 77.
31 1901 Census – Form A [http://www.census.nationalarchives.ie/reels/nai003680076/] [accessed 2 May 2014].
32 1911 Census – Form A [http://www.census.nationalarchives.ie/reels/nai000035936/] [accessed 2 May 2014].
33 1901 Census – Form B1 [http://www.census.nationalarchives.ie/reels/nai003680026/]; 1911 Census – Form B1 [http://www.census.nationalarchives.ie/reels/nai000035910/] [accessed 2 May 2014].
34 *Lepracaun*, July 1912.
35 *Irish Times*, 17 July 1912.

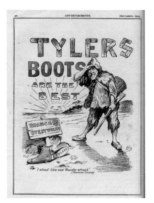

Advertisement for
Tyler's Boots by Thomas
Fitzpatrick. *The Lepracaun*
(Sept. 1905), p.90.

Advertisement for Mary
Fitzpatrick's illumination
business *The Lepracaun*
(Oct. 1912), p.64

and a Rathfarnham boot and floor polish firm selling 'Lepracaun Polish' demonstrates that it was not unusual practice at the time.[36] Nearly all of the *Lepracaun's* 122 issues were twenty pages in length, with Fitzpatrick never succeeding in an original ambition of turning the publication into a weekly venture.[37] Eager to 'spread light and laughter' throughout Ireland and paternally 'turn the search-light on the dark spots of municipal and provincial life, with a view to effecting a reform where necessary', the eponymous character of the *Lepracaun* (whose appearance sometimes varied) acted as the 'representative' of the rate-paying Irish public.[38]

With such an aspiration in mind Fitzpatrick bravely opted against accepting 'a substantial sum of money' from certain friends in high places at the time of the *Lepracaun's* founding, declining such assistance 'on the grounds that its acceptance might not leave him unfettered in his choice and treatment of subjects' portrayed in the journal.[39] The *Lepracaun* instead sought to raise additional income by advertising Fitzpatrick's own firm, which specialised in illuminated presentation addresses and Celtic artworks. One advertisement memorably featured the fictional publication *Public Opinion* claiming that 6 Upper Sackville Street produced the 'Finest Illuminated Work since the days of the Book of Kells'.[40] Mary Fitzpatrick trained under her father as an illuminating artist, and at a young age became a partner and subsequent inheritor of the family business. Her illuminated addresses were said to be designed 'in the highest style of illuminating Art', with the Lepracaun regularly reminding readers that her work was not produced in connection 'with any other address', seemingly a pointed reference to the fact that there was an older relative with the

---

36 'Lepracaun Cigarettes' were occasionally advertised in the
    Lepracaun, for example in its September 1906 issue. For a
    newspaper advertisement of the boot and floor polish firm in
    question see the *United Irishman*, 4 November 1905.
37 *Lepracaun*, May 1905.
38 Ibid.
39 Ibid., July 1912.
40 Ibid., June 1906.

same name and occupation operating from an address at 192 Clonliffe Road.[41] Until his health began to sharply decline in the early summer of 1911, at which point his eldest daughter took over the proprietorship of the journal, Thomas Fitzpatrick drew the black and white feature cartoons and commissioned illustrated advertisements in the *Lepracaun*. Subsequent cartoons were chiefly supplied by the London-based O'Hea ('SPEX') and Frank Reynolds ('SHY'), with occasional contributions from Mary Fitzpatrick herself and a few other less prominent artists such as Benjamin Bailey ('Ben Bay').

Cover of *The Lepracaun* (May, 1905).

O'Hea's identity as 'SPEX' has long been known. Evidence that 'SHY' was Reynolds relies on signatures attached to two original drawings which appeared in the *Lepracaun* and are stored in the National Library of Ireland: 'Bringing home the bride' [PD 2159 TX (39) 1] and 'In the Dublin Zoo' [PD 2159 TX (39) 2b]. In the 1911 English and Welsh census the London-born Reynolds, age 35, was recorded as living at 5 Market Place, Hertford.

In the *Lepracaun's* second issue Fitzpatrick warmly thanked his friends 'both of the public and the Press, metropolitan, provincial, and cross-Channel, for their magnificent reception' of the publication's debut number, assuring all concerned 'of his intention to leave nothing undone in the future to cater for their interest and amusement'.[42] His efforts did not go unrewarded. For example, the *Lepracaun's* September 1905 issue sold out on its day of publication, leaving 'thousands' of readers disappointed,[43] and by February 1906 it was being hailed as 'a model of what a humourous paper ought to be', succeeding as it did in providing mirthful illustrations and reading matter containing 'no sting or bitterness'.[44] Upon his death seven years later the *Evening Herald* had the following to say about Fitzpatrick's sprightly journalistic creation:

41 Ibid., Oct. 1914.
42 Ibid., June 1905.
43 Ibid., Oct. 1905.
44 Unidentified newspaper cutting loosely included within bound volumes of the *Lepracaun* formerly belonging to B. P. Bowen (Dublin City Library and Archive).

That brilliancy, so characteristic of the man, was fully exemplified in the "Lepracaun." From its inception the paper grew in popularity mainly by the aid of Mr. Fitzpatrick's pen. At times satirical, at moments even bitterly sarcastic (though there was no bitterness in the man himself, for above all, he possessed one of the most genial personalities in the world) on other occasions delightfully humorous, and with all the innate wit of the Celtic race, he was always the highest standard. In short, he brought to bear in the portrayal of his art all that was best in the branch to which he chose to devote himself. More could be said, but little more conveyed as to what Mr. Fitzpatrick did to raise the tone of what was generally known to the public as cartoons.[45]

The fact that the *Lepracaun* eclipsed in its lifespan all previous Dublin-based humorous journals is testament to the publication's popularity, with Fitzpatrick's ability to regularly combine joyful good humour with a discerning scorn of humbug and hypocrisy in public life crucial to ensuring its wide appeal.[46] Dealing largely with local politics and broader political matters from a Nationalist point of view,[47] in the *Lepracaun* it became Fitzpatrick's trademark to capture the essense of a political situation concerning Ireland in such a way that would both 'command the public mind and create endless mirth'.[48] He was still very fond of pointing out what he felt were the failings of John Redmond as a national leader, he actively demonstrated his 'dislike of Paddy jokes', and often equipped John Bull figures with 'bulging eyes and paunch and heavy jowls'.[49]

Fitzpatrick's central cover design, which was maintained for the entirety of the publication's circulation, 'was regarded as characteristic, almost rivalling the famous *Punch* cover by Richard Doyle (1824-83)'.[50] Surrounded by trees and shamrocks, it depicted a grinning leprechaun fervently entering copy atop his 'editorial mushroom' with the help of a team of mischievous imps. Of course, that it was a monthly rather than weekly journal gave Fitzpatrick and the *Lepracaun's* other contributors ample opportunity to come up with 'sprightlier gossip and more pointed political comment'.[51] Many of Fitzpatrick's *Lepracaun* cartoons were 'eagerly sought' after by readers, and his work was reproduced

---

45 *Evening Herald*, 16 July 1912.
46 See Bowen, 'Dublin Humorous Periodicals', pp 10-11.
47 Ibid., p. 11.
48 *Sunday Independent*, 21 July 1912.
49 Snoddy, *Dictionary of Irish Artists*, p. 161.
50 Ibid.
51 Curtis, *Apes and Angels*, p. 77.

in contemporary titles such as W. T. Stead's *Review of Reviews*.[52] Selected cartoons were also regularly published and snapped up in booklet form from 1906 until 1914. A unique monthly that was warmly received by critics and the general public alike, the *Lepracaun* cemented Fitzpatrick's reputation as one of the foremost black and white cartoonists of his day and left a lingering impression upon his death that he might have won himself more distinction as an artist 'had he chosen to employ his talents in a wider sphere than Ireland afforded'.[53]

Fitzpatrick's personality

Despite a somewhat 'retiring disposition', Fitzpatrick succeeded in making a host of friends throughout his life, admired as he was for his 'geniality', 'brilliant conversational powers' and perpetual 'fund of humourous stories'.[54] Also noted for his generosity, during the last fourteen or fifteen years of his life Fitzpatrick designed comic menu cards free of charge for social functions and annual conference dinners of the Irish Journalists' Association, an organisation of which he was a founding member, and the Dublin and Irish Association District of the Institute of Journalists.[55] Showcasing his 'delightful sense of humour', these immediately became highly prized souvenirs for attendees,[56] featuring 'kindly caricatures' of Fitzpatrick's journalistic colleagues which while occasionally 'severe', characteristically 'left no sting'.[57] Fitzpatrick also 'did some of his best work in the cause of

Photograph of Thomas Fitzpatrick, obituary in *Evening Telegraph*. (16 July 1912).

---

52 *Sunday Independent*, 21 July 1912.
53 Strickland, *A Dictionary of Irish Artists*, p.353. Strickland's observation brings to mind the opinion, expressed in 1883 by the British journal *St. Stephen's Review*, that Fitzpatrick's mentor John Fergus O'Hea could earn 'thousands per annum if he cared to live in London, where he is well known and highly thought of', instead of drawing 'his most marvellous cartoons for the most miserable of Irish comic papers'. See http://irishcomics.wikia.com/wiki/John_Fergus_O'Hea_(c._1838-1922) [accessed 2 May 2014].
54 *Freeman's Journal*, 17-18 July 1912; *Irish Times*, 17 July 1912; *Sunday Independent*, 21 July 1912.
55 *Irish Times*, 17-18 July 1912; *Freeman's Journal*, 18 July 1912.
56 *Sunday Independent*, 21 July 1912.
57 *Irish Times*, 17 July 1912.

Photograph of Thomas Fitzpatrick, obituary in *The Lepracaun* (July 1912), p.25.

charity', regularly contributing illuminated humorous programmes for use at fundraising events.[58] This habit was consistent with the artist's continual efforts to highlight the plight of the poor in his *Lepracaun* cartoons, a personality trait which did not go unnoticed by those whom he sought to help. A barefooted Dublin newsboy selling an evening paper, which on its front page announced Fitzpatrick's death and included one of the two photographs of the artist known to survive, pointed the face out to a customer inspecting the paper and declared 'There's our own man, sir'.[59]

Fitzpatrick's love of children and the kindness he exhibited towards those less fortunate than himself was addressed in his *Lepracaun* obituary:

> The claim of the hungry "street-arab" was allowed by him to the extent of his last copper, leaving him minus his tram fare, to walk home in the rain, and the beggar at his door took precedence in the first helping of his Christmas dinner. In the case of children, he was never so happy as when a collection of urchins was making chaos of his studio. On one occasion he was discovered discoursing a choice selection of dance music on a tin whistle to a juvenile audience seated on his work-table. On another he turned up at a friend's house, a considerable distance away, late one Christmas Eve night, a veritable Santa Claus, laden with toys for the children. At the seaside he revelled in carving sand-castles, and once constructed a wonderful Egyptian scene, with its pyramids, sphinx, etc., on an Irish strand, for the delighted "sand larks".[60]

---

58 Ibid.
59 *Sinn Féin*, 20 July 1912.
60 *Lepracaun*, July 1912.

Despite his talents and accomplishments Fitzpatrick was known to be a modest man, with his self-appreciation never extending beyond his uttering the words 'Not too bad', even when congratulated by 'his brother artists, men eminently capable of judging on the excellence of his work'.[61] Not that he was one shy to offer a negative opinion concerning the artistic work of others. When Irish-American sculptor Augustus Saint-Gauden's monument to Charles Stewart Parnell was erected at Upper O'Connell Street in 1911 Fitzpatrick denounced it as an 'unsightly deformity', typical of the 'rubbish' sometimes inflicted on the unfortunate public 'in the name of "high art"'.[62] The sculpture subsequently featured in an illustrated *Lepracaun* advertisement by Fitzpatrick for a nearby Dublin tobacco company, which saw a large lit 'Purcell's' cigarette on a plinth attracting the notice of Parnell and Lord Nelson on his pillar, thus forming 'three great Dublin monuments'.[63] Three years earlier Fitzpatrick had ridiculed the location of the Parnell monument as 'an obstruction to traffic' in a full-page *Lepracaun* cartoon, cleverly playing on words in relation to the late Home Rule leader's rising to prominence in 1877 by 'obstructing' the daily business of the House of Commons to highlight Irish issues.[64] Due to numerous requests the cartoon was reproduced in September 1911, with the *Lepracaun* announcing that it still stood over the sentiments expressed. In connection with Westminster, it should be noted that Fitzpatrick apparently 'never tired of denouncing the parsimony of the British Treasury in the matter of Irish art grants'.[65]

Fitzpatrick's illness and death

At an age when nature usually gave 'full maturity to powers in the domain in which he was one of the masters',[66] Fitzpatrick died at his home on 16 July 1912, his passing inflicting 'a major loss to the art of political cartoons in Ireland'.[67] The cause of death was officially listed as 'Neurosthenia (overwork)', which had been diagnosed some thirteen months earlier, and 'Paralysis asthenia', from which he had also suffered during the last thirteen weeks of his life.[68] In his will the artist left his grieving wife a personal estate worth £682 17s. 6d.[69]

---

61 Ibid.
62 Ibid.
63 Ibid., Mar. 1912. Nelson's Pillar was blown up by a left-wing republican splinter group in 1966.
64 Ibid., June 1908.
65 Ibid., July 1912.
66 *Freeman's Journal*, 18 July 1912.
67 Curtis, *Apes and Angels*, p. 81.
68 Thomas Fitzpatrick death certificate (General Register Office).
69 (National Archives of Ireland). This sum is equivalent to approximately €425,000 today.

The *Evening Herald* and *Evening Telegraph* were the first newspapers to break the news of Fitzpatrick's death. The *Herald* noted that Fitzpatrick 'had been in failing health for some time past, and had not been able to contribute to the [*Lepracaun*] journal with which his name will always be inseparably associated'.[70] In the *Telegraph* it was stated that although Fitzpatrick 'had been very ill for some months past', it had been hoped 'that his health would rally, and the news of his decease will come as a surprise to his many friends'.[71] The *Lepracaun* confirmed this information at the conclusion of its loving obituary published anonymously later that month:

> The death of Mr. Thos. FitzPatrick, the founder and proprietor of this journal, removes at once a distinguished artist and a man of broad sympathies from the world's stage ... To know "Fitz" was to love him. To the outsider who knew him not, he was the cynical critic whose pencil was as a white-hot iron searing all opponents with whom it came in contact. To his intimates he was a delightful personality, unspoiled and unspotted by the world; a man totally indifferent to self, and who regarded the poor as God's elect and the children as "Assurance of Heaven and its promise forever." ... A little over a year ago his friends observed with concern that his unusually robust health was gradually failing, the keen eye became dimmed, and the strong, steady hand lost its certainty. It was thought that a period of rest would have restored them to their old-time form, but as time went on the infirmity increased, notwithstanding the best skill and care of Dublin's most eminent specialists, until on July 16th, surrounded by his family, he passed peacefully away, and left his country the poorer by the loss of a gifted artist, a faithful friend, and a sterling Irishman: brilliant, fearless, golden-hearted "Fitz".[72]

Tributes

Generous tributes were paid to Fitzpatrick in a number of mainstream and radical Irish newspapers. When reporting on his death the *Sunday Independent* declared that Ireland, and in particular Dublin, had been left 'all the poorer'. The paper went on to offer the opinion that it was 'no idle tribute' to the late artist's memory to say that 'the sad news of Fitzpatrick's passing had been 'received with profound regret by all classes in the city, whom he so often delighted with his topical cartoons and

---

70 *Evening Herald*, 16 July 1912.
71 *Evening Telegraph*, 16 July 1912. The text of this obituary appeared in the *Telegraph's* sister title, the *Freeman's Journal*, the following day.
72 *Lepracaun*, July 1912.

his infinite fund of humour'.[73] The *Lepracaun* felt compelled, regarding the various obituaries of Fitzpatrick which appeared in the Irish press, to single out the following 'remarkable appreciation' in Sinn Féin's weekly organ:

> By the death of Thomas Fitzpatrick his country has been left, within the range of all the work that he attempted, poor indeed. In the matter of political cartoons, Ireland has from time to time produced artists of distinction, but with the exception of him who died this week none of them was unswervingly devoted to her own service. Born in a day when public activities of every kind and on every side were treated in an atmosphere of insincerity and make-believe, he kept a watchful eye on humbug, and struck at it without misgiving or a second thought of what men call prudence. We have not yet outlived that evil tradition, but Fitzpatrick has certainly quickened the pace of its disappearance. The time has not come to measure the service done towards the purifying of Irish public life by the "Lepracaun" in its short existence, but it must inevitably come.

> He could not be wealthy as the commercialism that is now so fashionable judges wealth, but he was certainly rich in the reckoning of the spotted sovereigns that ran past his hands without an effort to touch them.

> Outside critics will agree that Fitzpatrick was one of the cleanest and most direct line draughtsmen that this country ever knew. He worked with an economy that belongs only to the specially inspired. The smallest indication of a curve or the diminution of a line conveyed more than a labyrinth of scratchy tentative suggestions from a hand less confident. It fell to him to do much work that escaped notice or, at least, notoriety, but even here, however much he depreciated it himself, the note of genius sounded true. No unconsidered trifle that fell from Thomas Fitzpatrick's pencil could by any shadow of confusion be ascribed to an artist who thought less clearly and struck less boldly.

---

73   *Sunday Independent*, 21 July 1912.

One note can never be mistaken. In any issue where the interest of the poor arose their cause was paramount. Not in this way are commercial fortunes built. Deposuit potentes de sedibus, et exaltavit humiles ['He took down the mighty from their thrones, and lifted up the lowly'].[74]

The respect worked both ways and hinted at Fitzpatrick's politics. When *Sinn Féin* had experimented as a daily evening paper in late 1909, the *Lepracaun* made a point of wishing 'the fearless journal a long time' in existence.[75]

Funeral

Fitzpatrick was buried in the same (now unmarked) St. Bridget's plot at Glasnevin Cemetery as his late mother and first-born son.[76] On the evening of Wednesday 17 July his remains had been removed to St. Peter's Church, Phibsborough. Following mass the next morning, his body was then taken to Glasnevin for burial, followed by a large funeral cortege of 'colleagues and friends united in paying a last tribute to one whom they held in affectionate esteem'.[77] The requiem mass at St. Peter's Church was performed by Rathfarnham priest Rev. M. T. Bourke, who also conducted the funeral service at Fitzpatrick's graveside. Over one hundred and fifty names were listed as being present for the funeral according to one newspaper report the next day, including *Evening Herald* cartoonist Gordon Brewster and a number of politicians and public figures.[78]

Also present were delegations representing the Irish Journalists' Association and the Dublin and Irish Association District. A day earlier, the former's president M. M. O'Hara had remembered his late colleague as 'a journalist devoted to his colleagues in every way that he could do service,' a man whose 'genius kept company with his good will'. A previous president, J. B. Hall, seconded O'Hara's motion to formally pay their sympathy to Fitzpatrick's family, noting that 'no more melancholy duty had ever

---

74 *Sinn Féin*, 20 July 1912. For an abbreviated version see *Lepracaun*, July 1912.
75 *Lepracaun*, Oct. 1909.
76 On 6 November 2013 I received the following e-mail response from the late Shane MacThomáis of Glasnevin Cemetery in relation to a query, submitted the previous day, concerning Fitzpatrick's grave: 'I went up to the grave (RH 218.5) and it is unmarked, there is a foundation on it and it is possible that it was once marked but perhaps the headstone fell into disrepair. Alternatively it may have never been marked. Thomas Fitzpatrick owns the grave but the last burial in it was in 1919. Of the 1.2 million people here in Glasnevin about half are in unmarked graves. Unmarked graves would have been fairly prevalent in 1912 especially when the head of a family died'. Jim Fitzpatrick remembers visiting his grandfather's grave as a child, and that it was marked at the time. Jim Fitzpatrick interview with author (11 May 2014).
77 *Freeman's Journal*, 17 July 1912; *Irish Times*, 19 July 1912.
78 *Irish Times*, 19 July 1912.

fallen to his lot'.[79] During the Dublin and Irish Association District meeting held elsewhere in the city, meanwhile, a leading member, J. C. Percy, revealed that 'although he had differed with the artist on every subject under the sun, yet he loved and esteemed' Fitzpatrick, whose death he felt keenly. He went on to offer his opinion that Fitzpatrick's passing had deprived 'the whole circle of art in Ireland… of one of its most brilliant ornaments'. Count George Noble Plunkett seconded Percy's moving of a vote of condolence with Fitzpatrick's widow and children, paying tribute to the late artist's 'gift of being brilliant and witty without at the same time inflicting a wound'. Plunkett was speaking from personal experience. In 1907 he had been one of the many prominent local and national personalities given a full page profile with accompanying caricature treatment in the *Lepracaun*.[80] Plunkett poetically concluded his speech with the observation that Fitzpatrick's 'wit was like the summer lightning, which shed light around but never hurt'.[81]

"How happy could I be with either."

Count Plunkett cartoon by Thomas Fitzpatrick *The Lepracaun* (Sept. 1907), p.13.

Such a sentiment brings to mind a memorable anecdote about Fitzpatrick, which the *Lepracaun* included in its July 1912 obituary as evidence of how 'absolutely indifferent to praise or blame' from the subjects whom he portrayed in the publication's cartoons the artist had been:

> On one occasion, having caricatured a prominent politician of his acquaintance somewhat severely, he was unexpectedly accosted by the subject who, producing a copy of the paper, demanded indignantly – "What the divil did you do that for?"

---

79 *Freeman's Journal*, 18 July 1912.
80 *Lepracaun*, Sept. 1907.
81 *Irish Times*, 18 July 1912.

whereupon "Fitz," with a twinkle in his grey-blue eye, responded "What the divil did you deserve it for?" And then – the spectacle of cartoonist and cartooned marching off together arm-in-arm the best of friends.[82]

Final years of the *Lepracaun* and repeated family tragedy

In the aftermath of her father's death Mary Fitzpatrick, in addition to running the family illuminating art business at Upper Sackville Street, officially took over the proprietorship of the *Lepracaun*. She was an accomplished artist with tremendous drive, said to have 'inherited much of her father's genius',[83] and with help from firstly O'Hea and later Reynolds she succeeded in keeping the *Lepracaun* going for several more years. The journal's final issue appeared in February 1915, confirming problems producing its (missed) previous issue but showing no awareness that the end was nigh.[84]

This family disappointment would pale in significance compared to the wave of tragedy experienced at 10 Cabra Road shortly afterwards. In a four month period between late 1918 and early 1919 three of Thomas Fitzpatrick's children died during the great influenza epidemic and joined him in the Glasnevin Cemetery family plot, including Mary. The first to pass away was Thomas, an artist like his namesake father who seems to have contributed to the *Lepracaun* towards the end of its run. He died on 24 October 1918 from 'spinal paralysis', aged twenty. The second was Elizabeth ('Lilly'), a clerk, who died on 27 November 1918 from pneumonia. She was twenty-five. Both burials were organised by Mary, who would then pass away herself on 1 March 1919 from 'influenza acute septic pneumonia', aged twenty-eight. All three siblings were unmarried.

---

82 *Lepracaun*, July 1912.

83 *Sunday Independent*, 21 July 1912.

84 The *Lepracaun's* final issue concluded with the following notice from Mary Fitzpatrick: 'We regret delay in publishing our issue of January, but as it was a bit late in the month, and on the suggestion of our Agents, we now publish our February issue, and in future all issues will be published about 15th each month'. Above this was the usual advertisement for domestic and foreign subscriptions, and the information that the *Lepracaun* could be obtained direct from the editorial office at 6 Upper O'Connell Street, all railway bookstalls, and retail agents in Dublin, Cork and Liverpool. From its July 1913 issue the *Lepracaun* was printed by Cahill & Co. Ltd., 40 Lower Ormand Quay. It had previously been printed by Wood Printing Works, 13 Fleet Street.

Jim Fitzpatrick and the subsequent family artistic tradition

The fact that their younger brother James ('Jimmy') survived the influenza epidemic of 1918-19, however, has ensured that the Fitzpatrick artistic family tradition survives to the present day. In 1943 his wife Elizabeth ('Lilly'), remembered as 'an Empire loyalist, not the bigoted type',[85] gave birth to Jim Fitzpatrick, a well-known contemporary Irish artist.[86] Since the early 1970s Jim Fitzpatrick's art has sought mainly to bring 'the rich and colourful history and legends of Ireland to life', with a vast collection of original Celtic artworks celebrating the 'distinctive and unique ancient histories, myths and legends' of his native land. His career has also been 'hugely influenced by the power of Irish music and literature', and in the past he has collaborated with the likes of Thin Lizzy and Sinéad O'Connor.[87]

Photograph of Jim FitzPatrick in 1967
(Courtesy Jim FitzPatrick)

The artist is today best known for 'Viva Che', a red and black screen-printed poster of legendary South American revolutionary leader Che Guevara, which Jim Fitzpatrick designed in 1968 as a 'personal protest' against his brutal murder by the Bolivian government the previous year. The image spread across the world like wildfire to become, in his own words, 'an international symbol of resistance to oppression', something that fills its creator (who met Guevara in Ireland in 1962) with great pride.[88] After over four decades of allowing 'free and fair usage, for political purposes only' of 'Viva Che', in September 2011 Jim Fitzpatrick obtained the legal copyright to his iconic image, hoping to end its mass and crass commercial exploitation. He promptly transferred the copyright to Guevara's daughter Alieda 'on behalf of the Cuban people for posterity'.[89] Today, Jim's son Conann lectures in animation and design at Belfast College of Art, University of Ulster, meaning that Thomas Fitzpatrick has had several children, a grandson, and a great-grandson follow in his artistic footsteps. 'Not too bad'.

Jim FitzPatrick's iconic 'Viva Che'
(Courtesy Jim FitzPatrick)

---

85 Tommy Graham, 'Che Guevara, Jim Fitzpatrick and the making of an icon', in *History Ireland*, Vol. 16, No. 4 (July/August 2008), p. 52.

86 Jim Fitzpatrick's maternal grandparents also perished during the 1918-19 influenza epidemic. He recalls that when growing up 'the great flu was like the Holocaust in our house, it was not talked about in the family'. Jim Fitzpatrick interview with author (11 May 2014).

87 See http://www.jimfitzpatrick.com/myhome/welcome-to-the-art-of-jim-fitzpatrick/ [accessed 9 May 2014].

88 Ibid.

89 Ibid.

THE LEPRACAUN

VOL. I., No 1.   MAY, 1905.   PRICE ONE PENNY.

The Lepracaun—"Walk up Gentlemen! Walk up! the shows just a-goin' to begin! along with what ye'll see inside,
ye can see yerselves as others see ye, an' the price of the book is only a Penny."

The Lepracaun Cartoon Monthly by Ciarán Wallace

Attitudes and readership

In the opening address to his 'Fellow Countrymen' in May 1905 the fictitious Lepracaun described his new publication, and the readership he hoped to attract. In comically florid language he promised to spread laughter from the 'billowy retreat of the Clifden bivalve, to the noble bay where the Clupea Haregus Dublinenis disports its silvery radiance' – in other words from the Galway Bay oyster to the Dublin Bay herring. His main concern was with 'that … highly auriferous bird – The Ratepayer'. The editor's comically pompous verbosity, using terms like 'auriferous' (gold-bearing) and zoological names for common items, presumes that the reader understands such terms in order to get the joke. Evidently his readers got the joke and this tells us something about who read *The Lepracaun*, who worked for it and about society in Dublin at the time. With its mixture of local gossip and political cartoons, often based on Classical or Shakespearean references, *The Lepracaun Cartoon Monthly* attracted educated, middle-class readers and advertisers for a decade.

The period between 1905 when the magazine began and 1915 when it closed down was one of great social, political and technological change in Ireland. Following the 'Parnell spilt' the Irish Parliamentary Party (IPP) was reunited under the leadership of John Redmond, stirring fresh hopes of a Home Rule parliament in Dublin. The Ulster Unionist party was established in response to this threat. In Westminster the Liberal landslide of 1906 introduced a period of radical innovation in welfare across Britain and Ireland. Locally, Labour was evolving as a political force in Dublin Municipal Council and Sinn Féin, the new reform party, also won seats in City Hall. Around a dozen city councillors were unionists, while in the independent suburban town halls of Rathmines and Pembroke (modern day Ballsbridge and Donnybrook) unionists were in the majority. So cartoonists had lots of political material to work with. Major changes in Irish society gave them even more to laugh at; the position of women in the workplace, politics and innovations in transport, science and communications were all satirised in *Lepracaun* cartoons. But readers and cartoonists also laughed at the same things which amuse or frustrate us today. Politicians' pay, young people's fashions and family life all appear in the magazine's pages, although sometimes the figures (both financial and anatomical) from a century ago might amuse us for different reasons in this century.

From the literary references and social attitudes expressed in its articles, cartoons and advertisements *The Lepracaun* evidently appealed to the well-read, urban reader, who supported moderate nationalism, was interested in new technology but uneasy at the prospect of votes for women. The majority of

Dubliners were Roman Catholic, although the proportion of non-Catholics in the suburbs was higher than today.[90] Most *Lepracaun* readers were Catholic but they did not live in terror of their bishops. While matters of religion were treated with respect the magazine was not afraid to satirise the hierarchy if the church stepped into the realm of national politics. When, against the wishes of the party leadership, Cardinal Logue supported Tim Healy's bid to be the IPP candidate in the North Louth by-election of 1910, under his pen-name of 'Fitz' the magazine's founder and chief cartoonist, Thomas Fitzpatrick, drew a diminutive Healy cowering behind the skirts of Cardinal 'Richelieu' Logue. The image and caption, from Edward Bulwer Lytton's play 'Richelieu; or The Conspiracy' (1839), present Logue as arrogant and overweening.[91] Earlier, 'Fitz' had shown the cardinal's crozier about to crush *The Irish Peasant*, a Navan based paper whose strongly nationalist editorial line was matched by a robust anti-clericalism. As a satirist 'Fitz' was necessarily opposed to such censorship. Under pressure from the church the owners of *The Irish Peasant* closed the paper down.[92]

We know that James Joyce, the quintessential Edwardian Dubliner, read *The Lepracaun* as he mentions it in his letters. In 1905 he worried that a poem in *The Lepracaun* signed 'Joyce' might be mistakenly attributed to him. Writing from Rome in 1906 he mentioned receiving copies of the cartoon monthly and that other new publication *Sinn Féin*. He posted *The Lepracaun* to his brother Stanislaus in Trieste, so he was also a reader.[93] Joyce had an interest in satirical journals, in 1903 he had considered launching *The Goblin* as a 'merrily sinister contrast to the *Freeman's Journal*, *Irish Times* and *Daily Express*' but the plan never materialised.[94] Another *Lepracaun* reader was Seán T. O'Kelly, later cabinet minister, Tánaiste and President of Ireland. Like Joyce, Seán T. was a Dubliner in his early twenties when *The Lepracaun* was launched. Working as a business manager in the Gaelic League paper, *An Claideamh Soluis*, and campaigning for Sinn Féin, he believed that *The Lepracaun*

---

90 In 1911 the city's population was 83% Catholic while in the suburbs the figure was 63%. *Census of Ireland, 1911 Table XXIX*. There was a steady decline in the number of non-Roman Catholics between 1911 and 1926 nationally. Adrian Redmond, Mary Heanuc, 'Aspects of society' in Adrian Redmond (ed.) *That was then, This is now: change in Ireland 1899 – 1949: A publication to mark the 50th anniversary of the Central Statistics Office.* (Dublin, 2000), p. 55. For the 2011 demographic profile see 'Religion by County' in Central Statistics Office, *Profile 7: Religion, ethnicity and Irish Travellers* (Dublin, 2012) p.8.

91 *The Lepracaun*, Jan. 1910, p. 165. In an open letter Logue disingenuously wrote that it would not be in keeping with his position to actually nominate a candidate – 'otherwise I should willingly nominate Mr. Healy'. *Freeman's Journal*, 14 Jan. 1910, p. 7.

92 *The Lepracaun*, Jan. 1907, p. 402. Peter Murray, 'Lindsay Crawford's 'Impossible Demand'? The Southern Irish Dimension of the Independent Orange Project' in *National Institute for Regional and Spatial Analysis Working Paper Series*, (Feb. 2002), pp 9-10, http://www.maynoothuniversity.ie/nirsa/wp-content/uploads/2013/05/WPS05.pdf [consulted 13 Nov. 2014].

93 Richard Ellman (ed.), *Selected Letters of James Joyce* (London, 1975) pp 62-3, 127, 132-3.

94 Richard Ellman, *James Joyce: New and Revised Edition* (Oxford, 1982) p. 140.

helped to sway public opinion towards the new movement. In 1952, when he was president, he recalled it as 'a monthly humorous journal … which was rather sympathetic to Sinn Féin. It produced a number of cartoons … which had an influence in turning the minds of the people against the Parliamentary Party and to the Sinn Féin ideals'. O'Kelly identified a particular 'Fitz' cartoon about the North Leitrim by-election in 1908 as being 'most effective in this direction'.[95] He had reason to recall this particular illustration as he featured prominently in it, alongside Alderman Thomas Kelly and *Sinn Féin* editor Arthur Griffith. Curiously, the cartoon in question pokes fun at the losing Sinn Féin candidate, but the caption refers to the IPP's underhand tactics during the campaign and expresses some satisfaction at the new party's first attempt at national politics.

The North Leitrim by-election, Sinn Féin's first foray into national politics. *The Lepracaun* (Mar. 1908), p. 213.

In its gentle lampooning of all sides *The Lepracaun* had an almost universal appeal. This is evident in the regular press coverage which the cartoon monthly attracted. As a periodical aimed at the conventional nationalist middle-class IPP reader which also pleased Sinn Féin supporters, it is surprising how often *The Lepracaun* is mentioned in the *Irish Times*, a newspaper generally associated with unionist politics in this period. In its first year the *Irish Times* reviewed nine issues of the magazine and this coverage increased over the following two years. These reviews were short but very positive; 'With all its mirth there is no sting or bitterness…The Lepracaun is altogether a capital number',[96] and later 'its humour sparkles quite as merrily as ever'.[97] The frequency of these pieces, which were effectively free advertising, suggests that Fitzpatrick was calling in favours from fellow pressmen in the city. If this is the case, then his influence declined from 1908 to 1911 when the magazine was reviewed only twice per year. In 1912, the final year of Fitzpatrick's life, there were a dozen mentions of *The Lepracaun* one of which was a heartfelt obituary for 'Fitz' clearly

---

95 *Bureau of Military History Witness Statements*, Sean T. O'Kelly WS 1765 p. 38.
96 *Irish Times*, 24 Feb. 1906, p. 2.
97 *Irish Times*, 1 Nov. 1907, p. 5.

The British Empire presented as piracy in the Review of Reviews in 1906.

The Lepracaun (Apr. 1906), p.237.

written by a friend.[98] A second piece in the same edition of the *Irish Times* publicised the magazine's continuation beyond its founder's death by promoting the work of its remaining cartoonists.[99] It is less surprising that *The Lepracaun* received attention from the popular nationalist titles the *Freeman's Journal* and the *Irish Independent*. *The Freeman* represented the views of the IPP but it did not take notice of the party's witty monthly critic until August 1912 when it produced a very favourable review of *The Lepracaun's* special Horse Show issue.[100] The timing of this piece, just after Fitzpatrick's death, may reflect a desire to help the bereaved family as they struggled to maintain the business, but subsequent pieces in *The Freeman* are detailed and positive reviews evidently based on merit. The *Irish Independent* praised early issues of the magazine as 'lively' and 'delightful breezy satire'. More commercially useful was its comment 'for a penny it would be hard to get better value in pictures and letterpress'.[101] Provincial papers generally mentioned the magazine only when it referred to some local incident. *The Anglo-Celt* quoted a comic article on Cavan Rural District Council's discussion of the new cowshed regulations,[102] while the *Connaught Telegraph* relayed *Lepracaun* articles on the annual ball of the Kiltimagh Temperance Society and the activities of the Ballinrobe petty sessions.[103] *The Skibbereen Eagle*, however, maintained its reputation for taking the broader view with references to *Lepracaun* cartoons and articles on the controversy over compulsory Irish at the new National University and the IPP's attitude to the formation of the Irish Volunteers.[104]

---

98 *Irish Times*, 27 Jul. 1912, p. 4.
99 *Irish Times*, 27 Jul. 1912, p. 8.
100 *Freeman's Journal*, 24 Aug. 1912, p. 5.
101 *Irish Independent*, 13 Jul. 1906, p. 6; 12 Oct. 1908, p. 6.
102 *Anglo-Celt*, 11 Jun. 1910, p. 2.
103 *Connaught Telegraph*, 20 Apr. 1912, p. 4; 29 Mar. 1913, p. 4.
104 *Skibbereen Eagle*, 13 Sep. 1913, p. 1; 18 Jul. 1913, p. 7.

The readership of *The Lepracaun* stretched beyond Ireland and the Irish overseas, indeed its cartoons were still relevant long after the magazine ceased to trade. A *Lepracaun* cartoon satirising 'The Secret of England's Greatness' appeared in a prestigious British literary journal *The Review of Reviews* alongside leading cartoons from across the English-speaking world. Fitz's representation of John Bull as 'Buccaneer Bill' is described as 'perhaps the grimmest' treatment of British imperial greed.[105] In 1949, three decades after its closure, a *Lepracaun* cartoon appeared on the examination paper for the National University of Ireland. Students sitting for their B.A. in Irish were asked to compare the position of the language under the former Board of National Education as depicted in a 1905 cartoon, with its situation under the sarcastically labelled Ollscoil 'Naisiúnta' in 1949 (the 'National' University).[106] In 2013, on the centenary of the Dublin Lockout, *Lepracaun* illustrations from the period appeared in academic articles and popular exhibitions.[107]

Modernity and politics in 1907.
The Lepracaun (Sep. 1907), p.119.

As a humorous journal *The Lepracaun* gives us insights into political events but also into daily life in Dublin. A number of cartoons, for example, deal with Ulster unionist resistance to Home Rule, in many cases portraying unionism as a spoilt child refusing to do as he is told by a reasonable and coaxing nationalist adult. Understanding this attitude towards Ulster unionism in 1912 suggests that nationalists underestimated the extent of unionist opposition.

Modernity and politics in 1912.
The Lepracaun (May 1912), p.3.

105 *The Review of Reviews,* May 1906, pp 468, 473.
See *The Lepracaun,* Apr. 1906, p. 237.
106 Dónall Ó Cearráin, 'Tús na Troda: An Ghaeilge agus Ollscoil na hÉireann' in *Comhar,* Iml. 9, Uimh 1
(Jan, 1950), pp 5-7. Ó Cearráin used another *Lepracaun* cartoon 'When Doctors Differ' from June 1909 to support his case for strengthening the position of Irish in the university.
107 John White, 'Bad, sad specimens of the human race: Nationalist opinion and the striking workers of 1913' in *History Ireland,* Vol. 21, No. 4 (Jul./Aug. 2013), pp 34-6; Francis Devine (ed.) *A Capital in Conflict: Dublin City and the 1913 Lockout* (Dublin, 2013) pp 271, 313; 'The Dublin Lockout' exhibition at the National Library of Ireland, Kildare Street, Aug. 2013-Oct. 2014.

Cartoons also show us popular responses to new technology. Motor cars generally represent progress, independence and modernity in *The Lepracaun* but the speeding motorist appeared as early as 1908 when a cartoon suggested shooting these dangerous road-hogs (See p. 49). Innovations in transport provided much material for comedy with early bi-planes and enormous airships featuring in 1912 and 1913.[108] As early as 1907 an advertisement used an image of space travel to promote Anti-Laria non-alcoholic wine ('a stimulant rivalled only by champagne at a fraction of the cost').[109] Bicycles may have been less exciting than fizzy drinks from Mars, but they appeared regularly in advertisements and cartoons. Allowing Dubliners the freedom to travel further and faster, the bicycle was another symbol of modernity and independence but at a fraction of the price of a motor car. The invention of the inflatable tube and rubber tyre presumably added to the appeal. Dublin's new electricity supply gave the cartoonists another useful topic and readers could enjoy *The Lepracaun* by the light of their new electric lamps. The telephone and phonograph also entered common use during this decade so they too became subjects for satire. As Dubliners flocked to the novelty of cinema so the writers and artists in the magazine lampooned city's politicians as cowboys and bank-robbers on the big screen.[110]

All periodicals depend on advertising and *The Lepracaun* was successful in attracting many reliable repeat advertisers. Kennedy's bread featured regularly on the back cover, with an image of bread being sliced or sturdy children clambering onto a giant loaf, but other advertisements tell us more about Dublin life.[111] Drapers, department stores and shoe-shops advertised very regularly but it is the number of advertisements for jewellery, music, photography and artworks which stands out. Of the various products and services appearing in the magazine these are among those most frequently advertised. Other commonly featured notices came from hoteliers and insurance companies, indicating the economic standing of the magazine's readership. The most common category of advertisement, however, was for public houses and brands of drink. Gleeson's of the North Circular Road and The Hut in Phibsboro were not far from Fitzpatrick's home in Glasnevin so it is possible that some mutual patronage was involved, but pubs across the city promoted their reserve whiskey or hot food. Many advertisements were drawn by 'Fitz', so in some issues almost every illustration comes from his pen. Special Christmas editions carried more advertisements and for a wider range

---

108 *The Lepracaun*, May 1912, p. 5; Mar. 1913, p. 131.
109 *The Lepracaun*, Jul. 1907, p. 38.
110 *The Lepracaun*, Feb. 1914, p. 267.
111 This latter image reappeared some years later in the satirical *Dublin Opinion*, Dec. 1923, p. 262, as cited in Anne Dolan, 'Fumbling in the greasy till: Dublin Opinion and the Irish bourgeoisie, 1922-23' (M.A. thesis, University College Dublin, 1996) p.171 n. 103.

of up-market items, but it was the bumper Horse Show editions that promoted the most expensive goods. For this lucrative market *The Lepracaun* made a rare change for its September 1909 cover, presenting a cartoon of a stylish young lady perched rather precariously on the back of a lordly centaur, with cigar, monocle and top-hat. His waistcoat is emblazoned with 'L.S.D.' for pounds, shillings and pence, a reference to the economic importance of the show to the city and all its traders – including *The Lepracaun* (See p. 67).[112]

While nationalist in tone, *The Lepracaun's* cartoons and advertisements appealed to a range of political outlooks. However, two groups which might not have enjoyed its style of wit were women and the Labour movement. The magazine took a conventional view on women's role in society. Presenting younger women as fashion victims in outrageous hats or hobble-skirts, the editor did not expect them to pursue a career, and certainly not once they had fulfilled their primary mission of getting married. A cartoon in April 1910 of a 'lady-teacher', leaving her husband with the baby while she goes out to work, accompanied an article about the over-supply of teachers. The editor demanded that married female teachers be called upon to resign in order to create vacancies. Older women in *The Lepracaun* generally fell into two types, the uncouth tenement woman and the comical spinster. Middle-class matrons rarely appeared. Working-class women were funny because they failed to behave as the 'gentler sex'. In December 1907 for example, despite the sign 'No ladies supplied at this bar' two witty women point out that they do not require 'ladies' but whiskey.[113] Elsewhere, using inversion for comic effect, a violent wife orders her frightened husband to mind their tenement room while she goes out socialising with her friends.[114] The 'old-maid' type is shown trying out a 'bust developer' medicine with disastrous effects to her face.[115] Another version of the spinster is the suffragette. Between 1910 and 1913 a number of cartoons appeared in the magazine about the women's suffrage campaign. Ireland did not experience the level of radicalism and destruction of property seen in Britain but, from coverage in the press and on newsreels, the public were well aware of the dramatic events transpiring across the Irish Sea. Arguably, *The Lepracaun's* depictions of suffragettes were less offensive than those in British publications, but they were far from supportive.

Labour, the other group who may not have appreciated the humour, emerged as a political force in the city around the time *The Lepracaun* first appeared. Radical electoral reforms in 1898 allowed many more working-class Dubliners to vote, and for the first time workers' representatives could stand for

---

112 *The Lepracaun*, Sep. 1909, p. 65.
113 *The Lepracaun*, Dec. 1907, p. 159.
114 *The Lepracaun*, Aug. 1910, p. 45.
115 *The Lepracaun*, Apr. 1908, p. 230.

election. A 1905 'Fitz' cartoon satirised the unkempt Labour candidate leaving his semi-derelict tenement to go to the election count. Embarrassed at his wife calling from an upper window he tells her to 'Go in out o' that, for hiven's sake, if ye ever want to be a Lady Mayoress'.[116] Such class-based comedy, however, soon turned into reality when Joseph Nannetti was elected Lord Mayor in 1906 on a Labour ticket. *The Lepracaun* need not have feared imminent socialism in City Hall, Nannetti was soon absorbed into the IPP and ended his career as a 'rather mild sort of radical'.[117] Following a railway strike in 1911 John Fergus O'Hea, using the pen-name 'SPEX,' drew a cartoon entitled 'After the battle', showing a cold and starving family huddling beneath hollow strike slogans while union organisers tucked into a hearty meal complete with cigars and champagne; the leadership grew fat while their misled members paid the price (See p. 187).[118] During the Lockout, or General Strike, of 1913 some *Lepracaun* cartoons portrayed both workers and employers as equally at fault, with the public and poor suffering the consequences. But trade unions were generally less favourably treated being presented, in March 1913 for instance, as the mad March hare leading the workers astray (See p. 191).[119]

In contrast to its sceptical treatment of women or workers attempting to enter the political world, *The Lepracaun* consistently attacked elected politicians and appointed officials who failed in their responsibilities to the poor. It was especially severe on those who neglected children. Portly policemen chasing juvenile fruit-sellers off the street, cemetery administrators charging high prices for wretched pit burials and corrupt traders selling watered-down milk to an impoverished family all felt the sting of the cartoonist's pen. Poor Law Guardians, responsible for administering the rudimentary social welfare system of the day, came in for particular criticism. Described as 'Bumble' after the cruel workhouse master in Dickens' *Oliver Twist* these notoriously inefficient and crooked officials, and the system which employed them, fuelled the editor's reforming zeal. Articles and cartoons satirised their unfair hiring policy, their reluctance to buy Irish-made produce and the short rations which they gave to workhouse inmates. Little wonder that 'Fitz' gave such a wholehearted welcome to the introduction of the Old Age Pension in his New Year cartoon for January 1909. An elderly couple are shown receiving their first pension, in the background is the 'workhouse of misery … the curse of Ireland' and a tombstone marking the passing of a system which was 'a happy home

---

116 *The Lepracaun*, Oct. 1905, p. 115.
117 James McConnel, 'Fenians at Westminster: the Edwardian Irish Parliamentary Party and the legacy of the New Departure', *Irish Historical Studies*, 34: 133 (May 2004), 42-6. For more on Nannetti see Ciarán Wallace, 'Joseph P. Nannetti, Lord Mayor 1906-08:"a rather mild sort of rebel"' in Ruth McManus & Lisa-Marie Griffith (eds), *Leaders of the city: Dublin's first citizens, 1500–1950* (Dublin, 2013).
118 *The Lepracaun*, Nov. 1911, p. 243.
119 *The Lepracaun*, Mar. 1913, p. 135.

for contractors, officials, guardians and loafers. But a hell for the poor.' In a rare instance of Irish praise for the United Kingdom Treasury the elderly woman says 'God love … them that sent it' (See p. 59). [120]

We cannot pretend to know the full range of people who picked up a copy of *The Lepracaun* at a newsstand or found one left behind on a tram, or who passed copies to a friend or left them lying around the house for visitors. What we do know is that, in a publishing market where the average satirical journal survived only a few years, Thomas Fitzpatrick's venture lasted a decade.[121] This proves that it struck a chord with many Dubliners, both readers and advertisers. The fact that *The Lepracaun* was cited in the national and provincial press, appeared in the *Review of Reviews* and was still being mined for material decades later is a testament to the quality of its content. But what did the reader get for their penny a month? The next section looks at the facts and figures, describing the layout of the magazine and listing the other cartoonists who worked on it. The life and career of Thomas Fitzpatrick, *The Lepracaun's* founder, editor and most prolific cartoonist, is described in the preceding essay by James Curry.

The introduction of the Old Age Pension. *The Lepracaun* (Jan. 1909), p.59.

120 *The Lepracaun*, Jan. 1909, p. 179.
121 Contemporaneous comic publications included: *The Quiz*, May – October 1915 (6 months); *Irish Fun*, 1915-26 (11 years); *The Lepracaun*, 1905-15 (10 years); *The Irish Figaro*, 1898-1901 (3 years); *The Jarvey*, 1889-90 (1 year); *Pat*, 1879-83 (4 years); *Zoz*, 1876-78 (2 years); *Ireland's Eye*, 1874-82 (8 years). Anne Dolan, 'Fumbling in the greasy till: Dublin Opinion and the Irish bourgeoisie, 1922-23' (M.A. thesis, University College Dublin, 1996) p. 143 n. 6.

Contents, cartoonists and successors

A typical edition of *The Lepracaun* had sixteen pages, black and white, measuring 21 cm wide by 27.5 cm deep. Almost half of each issue was devoted to advertisements (many illustrated by Fitzatrick), 40% was cartoons with the remaining space being short articles, jokes or snippets of gossip. Surrounding the front page image of the Lepracaun at his 'editorial musharoom' [sic] were smaller advertisements for products like Tyler's shoes, Prescott's dye works or Dichronic Ink - 'the best for all fountain pens'. The back cover carried a full-page advertisement, usually for Kennedy's bakery, and a number of inside pages were divided among six or eight smaller advertisements. A wide range of firms used the magazine to promote their wares or services. M.H. Gill booksellers, Robert Wilson's Cycles and Jules & Co. Coiffure de Paris may no longer be in business, but Brown Thomas, Clery's, and *Ireland's Own* magazine are all still trading. The most common advertisements were for pubs, then drapers and shoe shops, with jewellers and tobacconists also appearing regularly.

Most monthly issues had at least two full-page cartoons with smaller comic illustrations liberally scattered through the other pages. Across its ten year run *The Lepracaun* cartoonists had favourite topics for their satire. Unsurprisingly, politics was the most popular theme with much to satirise at home in Dublin and in Westminster. The campaign for Home Rule and the resistance of Ulster Unionists provided a reliable source of material, with the activities of the Liberal government, the 'People's Budget' of 1909 and the behaviour of the British Empire filling any gaps. Cartoons about life in Dublin accounted for almost as many pages as politics, with rich pickings among issues of social class, law and order and public health. John Redmond, leader of the IPP, was the most frequently caricatured politician, barely rivalled by Prime Minister H.H. Asquith with half as many appearances. Other individuals, whether elected representatives like Tim Healy, William O'Brien and Edward Carson or prominent administrator and businessmen such as Dublin Town Clerk Henry Campbell, art collector and philanthropist Hugh Lane or Gaelic activist Douglas Hyde, received barely a quarter of the attention devoted to Redmond, with senior clerics appearing even less frequently. But the range of cartoon topics was far wider than this short list suggests. From agriculture and air travel through motor cars and music to weather and whiskey *The Lepracaun* cartoonists kept a close eye on all aspects of daily life.

The magazine's most prolific cartoonist by far was Thomas Fitzpatrick himself, producing all of the content from its foundation until November 1908. Apart from his illustrations for advertisements he drew a total of 506 attractive and perceptive cartoons between 1905 and his death in 1912. The first to join 'Fitz' was John Fergus O'Hea (SPEX), a Cork artist who had been the skilled principal cartoonist in *Zozimus*, *Ireland's Eye*, *Zoz*, and *Pat*.[122] O'Hea did much of the work on the *Weekly Freeman* before joining *The Lepracaun* in late 1908 where his more modern style appeared in almost one hundred cartoons by December 1914 when his work stops, possibly due to financial troubles in the dying months of the magazine. In May 1912 Frank Reynolds (S.H.Y.) began working for the magazine, creating 186 excellent cartoons up to August 1914. These three formed the nucleus of the creative team until 1912 and Fitzpatrick's illness and subsequent death. Reynolds and O'Hea carried on with occasional additions from others. A single piece in April 1913 did not result in V.L. O'Connor becoming a regular contributor, but Benjamin Bailey (Ben Bay) stayed with the publication from July to November 1914, producing some stylish cartoons. Between December 1914 and January 1915 the individualistic (and occasionally grim) pen of George Monks produced six cartoons, alongside three from Tom Lalor in the December 1914 edition. These final few months of business were evidently a period of some stress for *The Lepracaun* as it tried out a number of new cartoonists, carrying single examples of cartoons by 'McLean' in November 1914 and J.J. O'Reilly in January 1915. It was during this time that Mary Fitzpatrick, daughter of Thomas, began drawing for the magazine, along with her brother Thomas junior. Mary's work first appears in September 1914 with a pair of mournful reflections on the European war which had just begun. She reused some of her late father's ideas but the satire has less force and her dozen drawings do not demonstrate the skill which had taken 'Fitz' a lifetime to hone. Her younger brother was seventeen years old when he began working for the family firm in November 1914. His juvenile works show some potential but, like his older sister, a mere six cartoons over three months did not allow him to develop his craft.

Despite the Great War and its hardships Dublin still needed a laugh and within months of *The Lepracaun* closing a new comic journal emerged under the title of *Irish Fun*. It differed from Fitzpatrick's publication by concentrating on text rather than cartoons, a reflection perhaps of the high cost of employing skilled cartoonists as well as sharp writers. Its extended articles in Irish show an editorial line much closer to the Irish-Ireland vision of Sinn Féin, but some continuity is evident in its advertising. Hopkins and Hopkins, 1 Lower Sackville Street (O'Connell Street), purveyors of Irish art jewellery, placed an advertisement in the first edition. This simple text-only notice was quite unlike their regular advertisement in *The Lepracaun* with its illustration of an Irish warrior by 'Fitz', engraving of the Tara brooch and Celtic scrollwork border.[123] While the same printing block used in *The Lepracaun* was not transferred to *Irish Fun* the jeweller clearly hoped to reach the same

---

122 B.P. Bowen, 'Dublin Humorous Periodicals of the 19th Century' in *Dublin Historical Record*, Vol. 13, No. 1 (Mar. - May, 1952), p. 9. O'Hea died in 1922.

123 *Irish Fun*, Oct. 1915, p. 9. See *The Lepracaun*, Aug. 1908, p. 68 for an example of the more elaborate 'Fitz' advertisement.

readership through the new magazine. In the third edition Kennedy's bakery, a major advertiser with Fitzpatrick, also placed a basic unillustrated advertisement in *Irish Fun*. The mediocre quality of draughtsmanship in its early cartoons, and their scarcity, demonstrated the different focus of *Irish Fun*. It took a few years before a more directly comparable successor to *The Lepracaun* emerged. In 1922 *Dublin Opinion* appeared on the city's newsstands, with its balance of excellent cartoons and witty articles it was fitting heir to the tradition established by Fitzpatrick. Launched during the Civil War and produced by a fresh team of writers and cartoonists unconnected to its predecessor, *Dublin Opinion* addressed a very similar readership. Urban, middle class and conventionally nationalist readers laughed at much the same topics parodied in *The Lepracaun*. Through all the changes wrought by 1916, the War of Independence and Civil War, commerce carried on with Kennedy's bakery placing full page advertisements in the new comic monthly, reusing a 'Fitz' engraving first seen in *The Lepracaun*.[124]

For ten years Fitzpatrick's Lepracaun lived up to the promise he made on the platform back in 1905, 'to interest and amuse from month to month' and he had, according to his own judgment, supported 'every effort and movement for the benefit and progress of my country'.[125] With reformist zeal his team of cartoonists had shown up political chicanery, official obfuscation and administrative inefficiency of every sort. At a time of heightened tensions there was little of the pure (or puritanical) *fíorghael* about it. The pages of the cartoon monthly reveal a wry, urban sense of humour, able to poke fun at nationalists, unionists and separatists, workers and employers, suffragists and the Gaelic Revival in equal measure. Through its clever and skilful cartoons we can see a modern and cosmopolitan Dublin whose rising middle class were never allowed to take themselves too seriously.

124 *Dublin Opinion*, Dec. 1923, p. 262.
125 *The Lepracaun,* May 1905, p. 5.

Society

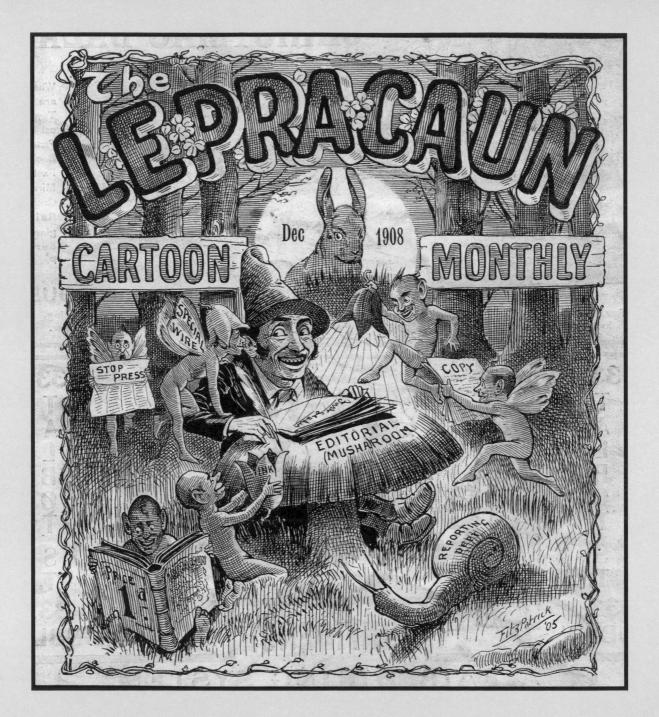

Fitz used the same cover illustration for regular editions of *The Lepracaun*, only changing it on rare occasions for a special Dublin Horse Show edition. As a lifelong pressman he incorporates the feel of a newsroom as the editor works through the night, receiving scandalous whispers by 'special wire' and shocking 'stop press' revelations. In what must be an insiders' joke, the reporting department crawls along at a snail's pace. But the busy scene is set in a moonlit wood with many folklore elements. The Lepracaun himself, the traditional figure of Irish fairy stories, is surrounded by his elven helpers. Fitz was an excellent draughtsman and some of the faces are very individualistic, presumably he had particular colleagues in mind when he drew them. The 'Editorial Musharoom' plays on Irish pronunciation, and like a juicy news story mushrooms appear overnight as if by magic (and often from manure!). The staring hare silhouetted against the full moon is a slightly sinister presence, both have deep mythological associations with unpredictable or flighty behaviour – and with madness.

To launch his new magazine Fitz begins with a political rally. With typical politician's modesty the Lepracaun urges the public to choose 'the greatest man the world has ever seen' - himself. The cartoon gives the atmosphere of a typical rally – a cheering crowd and a platform speaker surrounded by the great and the good. The dignitaries include the Lord Lieutenant Lord Aberdeen, with his excellent moustache; the bald Walter Long, Chief Secretary for Ireland; Horace Plunkett with a paper from the newly-formed Irish Department of Agriculture and Technical Instruction; Arthur Griffith, then editor of the *United Irishman*; nationalist MPs Willie Redmond, Tim Harrington, John Dillon and William Field, and the Lord Mayor Joseph Hutchinson with his chain of office. In the background the unkempt hair and fur collar of a young W.B. Yeats stick up, while the aged judge Chief Baron Palles, wig askew, peers out from the back row. Another legal wig identifies the profile of Timothy Healy MP with his dark beard and the City Swordbearer beside him in his ceremonial beaver-fur hat. To the right, through the small lenses of his pince-nez spectacles, the bearded stockbroker and patron of the arts Laurence 'Larky' Waldron stands between the profiles of Town Clerk Henry Campbell, with his white hair and dapper moustache, and Alderman Tom Kelly of Sinn Féin, with his full head of dark hair. The top right figure may be Stephen Ronan, a prominent barrister while, off the platform at the bottom right, Fitz has labelled himself as an enthusiastic member of the crowd. The absence of any women from the gathering tells us something about politics and public life at the time.

Fellow Countrymen.
May 1905, p.5

The Lepracaun did not hold the legal profession in particularly high regard, regularly satirising solicitors, barristers and judges (but never to the point of libel). In a series considering 'Our Un-Natural History' Fitz shows a group of legal vultures who have picked their victim's skeleton clean. Perhaps to avoid a similar fate, he only draws those vultures labelled as solicitors and barristers (King's Counsel) gripping bones marked 'L.S.D.' (for pounds, shillings and pence). The vulture depicted on the judges bench is clearly above such pecuniary considerations.

JUSTICE IS SATISFIED.

A BRIEF INTERVAL FOR REST AND REFRESHMENT.

Justice is satisfied. A brief interval for rest and refreshment.
January 1906, p. 179

St Patrick's Day was made an official holiday in 1903, but a debate soon arose over whether pubs should shut to avoid drunkenness on Ireland's national day. Patrick Pearse chaired a public meeting hosted by the Gaelic League at which representatives of Sinn Féin and Labour called for pub closures.[126] The pub trade was closely linked to the Irish Parliamentary Party so there was a political element to the dispute. Here Robert Russell of the Licensed Grocers & Vintners Protection Association performs impressive acrobatic tricks with a beer barrel as he tries to avoid the loss of business to his members. The Intoxicating Liquors (Ireland) Act, 1906, introduced Sunday closing but St. Patrick's Day drinking continued until the Intoxicating Liquor Act of 1927 which remained in force for sixty years.

---

126 *Irish Times*, 13 Mar. 1906, p.3

THE RUSSELL MANIFESTO(E).

The Russell Manifesto(e).
March 1906, p. 239

In common with society across Europe, casual anti-Semitism was part of Irish culture in the early twentieth century. Pogroms against the Jewish population in Russia had produced a new immigrant population from eastern Europe and the Baltic region. Here Fitz shows Pat, the Irishman, as a fly caught in the money-lender's web. Wearing a heavy gold chain with a seal, and multiple hats (perhaps suggesting a Jewish presence in many different businesses) the spider is labelled with 'L.S.D.' for pounds, shillings and pence. Exorbitant interest rates in the top left corner are accompanied by Fitz's satirical look at the names of some Jewish-owned financial firms. The lenders hope to hide their real identities, he claims, by using Irish names such as the *Céad Míle Fáilte* loan society and by employing a 'Gaelic speaking manager'. However, Fitz's own business acumen is evident in the adverts which *The Lepracaun* carried for H. Weiner & Co, a Jewish-owned hire-purchase firm, in 1908.

The Money-Lender.
April 1906, p. 239

Fitz was unlikely to sympathise with solicitors' complaints that their profession was becoming overcrowded. This poor solicitor, blind to honesty, has killed his client (the goose with the golden eggs) with his fees listed on the wall behind him. Items from £20 (for a five minutes consultation with a barrister) to 3 shillings and 6 pence (saluting a client) do not quite add up to the murderous total of £46, 5 shillings and 4 pence. Fitz's opinion of the clients who tolerate these prices is evident from their names on the legal case - 'Numbskull v Dunderhead'.

The goose with the golden eggs.

April 1906, p. 235

It is difficult for us today to appreciate the shock which the arrival of the motor car must have been on the streets of Dublin. Noisy, fast and dangerous a car bears down on the reader, its headlamp-eyes matching the monstrous expressions on the faces of the motorists.

The Road - Hog.
May 1906, p. 259

In their speeding vehicle emblazoned with the skull and crossbones the goggle-eyed motorists run over pedestrians, and just miss a mother and child. Amongst the dust and dirt which they stir up are 'microbes'—showing a modern awarenss of bacteria and disease. In the top right corner, most prominent of all, is *The Lepracaun's* startling remedy – a revolver.

"DON'T HESITATE TO SHOOT."

An influentially signed memorial has been addressed by the Road Union to the Prime Minister calling the attention of the Government to the grave and increasing evils caused by road-motor traffic.
The Lepracaun suggests an effective remedy.

Don't hesitate to shoot.
August 1908, p 61

Cultural nationalism and the growing Irish-Ireland movement challenged the Irish Parliamentary Party's hold on public opinion. Miss Erin is clearly smitten by the dashing (and wealthy) Doctor Douglas Hyde, just returned from a successful trip to America raising funds for his Gaelic League. Her former beau, poor John Redmond with his turf-cutter's slean labelled 'promises' and 'great expectations', must cling to the hope that his future riches under Home Rule will win her back. The cartoon appeared six month before Synge's production of 'The Playboy of the Western World' at The Abbey Theatre, so the western setting, rival lovers and the infamous slean are presumably purely coincidental.

JILTED.

JOHN REDMOND, M.P.—Bedad! I see how he's put the com'hether on her—he's earning more nor I am. But wait till I get me new holdin', "Home Rule," an' see if she won't be comin' back.

Jilted.
July 1906, p. 293

A dispute arose between the autocratic Catholic Bishop of Limerick, Edward Thomas O'Dwyer, and the Christian Brothers over control of a school in Bruff, Co. Limerick. To the displeasure of the locals the bishop was victorious and the Brothers withdrew from the school. In 1907 the Catholic hierarchy felt under threat from the radical separation of church and state in France, and the new English Education Bill (supported by John Redmond and his party) which weakened clerical control of schools. In this cartoon a self-confident Catholic and nationalist Fitz satirises Bishop O'Dwyer, armed with his crozier, mitre and robes, bullying Redmond – the elected nationalist leader, and trampling on the work of parliament, while the ruins of Bruff Christian Brothers' School stands accusingly in the background. 'Irish Clemenceaus' refers to George Clemenceau, the French politician responsible for a 1905 law reducing the power of the church.

"THE LAST SIEGE OF LIMERICK."

"I do not think that any Irish Bishop need have any grave apprehension on account of the irreligious blackguardism which any Irish Clemenceau may attempt to bring to bear against him. . . . As far as I can judge, the Irish Party have nothing behind them. They represent no opinion—Catholic or Irish—but are the puppets of the English Liberals in this matter."
—*Extract from the Bishop of Limerick's Letter to the "Freeman's Journal," 15th Dec., 1906.*

The last siege of Limerick.
January 1907, p. 401

Publicans within the 'Loop-line' railway, the City of Dublin Junction Railway Viaduct (opened in 1891) which encircles the docks and Sheriff Street area, commonly sold beer to dock-workers at the discounted price of 1½ pence a pint. Much to the alarm of the dockers (and the satisfaction of the rest of Dublin's publicans) the Recorder of Dublin, a senior figure in the city's judiciary, warned against the practice. Fitz shows the cheaper pint about to take a long drop watched by the Recorder, and by Robert Russell of the Licensed Grocers' and Vintners' Protection Association accompanied by members of the drinks trade. Weeping prisoners peer over the wall and wonder how they will wonder how they will afford a pint when released to resume their criminal careers along the quays.

LOOPING THE LOOP-LINER.

"Therefore, it is very much to be regretted that so high a judicial functionary as the Hon. the Recorder is should take sides with the one or the other. Does his lordship want to 'prevent a man from doing what he has a legal right to do?' Those traders, so much maligned, number about a dozen, and their only offence is that they sell a pint of beer to the workingman a halfpenny less than the other traders—which there is no law to prevent—and it is well known that not a few of the grocers and vintners' body sell rum, cordials, and other commodities under the customary trade prices, and that some of their most respectable members were not long since 'loop-liners.'"—Extract from letter of "Loop-Liner," *Evening Telegraph*, October 21st.

Looping the Loop-Liner.
November 1907, p. 127

The Licensed Grocers' & Vintners' Protection Association was a frequent target of Fitz's pen, but here he stabs at the power of the Guinness Brewery and the monopoly it imposed on the drink trade. To sell Guinness the publican had to agree not to stock any competitor's 'extra stout, porter or other brown beer'. 'Bung' in the caption implies a bribe or any financial corruption. The greedy James's Gate monster wears a peer's coronet, reminding readers of Edward Cecil Guinness who was created Viscount Iveagh in 1905, (subsequently becoming the 1st Earl of Iveagh in 1919). *The Lepracaun* often highlighted the unionist politics of the Guinness family, and here Fitz satirises their exclusive hiring practices as they seek an engineer who 'must be a gentleman by birth'. The damage caused by the brewing giant to the smaller breweries is shown in the abandoned factory behind the ensnared publican.

The Bung Frankenstein, or the Collar of Gold.

August 1908, p. 77

The Lepracaun greeted each new year with an appropriate cartoon and for 1909 Fitz was evidently delighted to welcome the introduction of the Old-Age Pension, a radical expansion of state welfare introduced by David Lloyd George, the Liberal Chancellor of the Exchequer. The elderly couple receiving the good news have been saved from the indignity and cruelty of the workhouse, in operation since the 1840s. In drawing a headstone for 'Bumble', the heartless beadle who ran the workhouse in Dickens' *Oliver Twist*, Fitz bids farewell to a corrupt and outdated system.

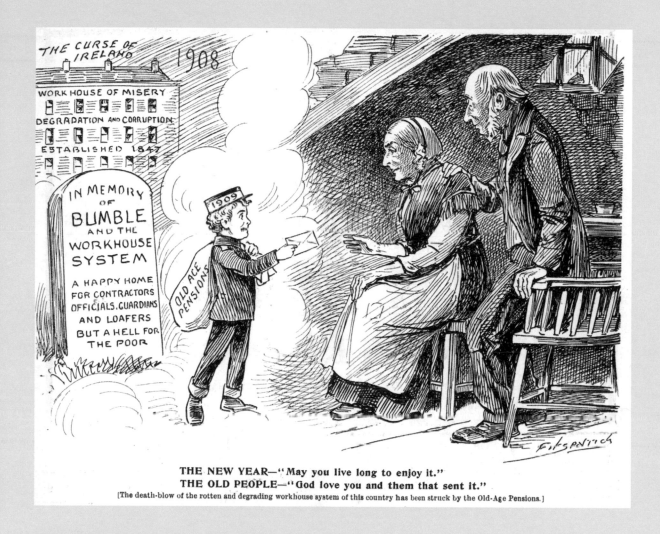

THE NEW YEAR—"May you live long to enjoy it."
THE OLD PEOPLE—"God love you and them that sent it."
[The death-blow of the rotten and degrading workhouse system of this country has been struck by the Old-Age Pensions.]

January 1909, p. 179

After years of effort Ireland was finally to have a National University which was acceptable to the Catholic majority. A controversy arose over whether the Irish language should be a compulsory subject for entrants to the university; Dr Douglas Hyde of the Gaelic League campaigned for compulsory Irish against the opposition of the Jesuit Dr William Delany, Dublin councillor Dr James McWalter and Stephen Gwynn. In this cartoon the National University train, driven by a bishop, speeds down the line but risks being derailed by the compulsory Irish dispute. This is the first instance of Irish speech appearing in a *Lepracaun* cartoon, as Hyde warns the Irish language donkey '*Bí anso chugham! Muinfead-sa béarla duit*' (Come here to me! I'll teach you English). However, Fitz may not have known much Irish as *béarla*, the word for English, is misspelt in the Gaelic script.

When Doctors differ, then comes the Tug-o'-War.

When Doctors differ, then comes the Tug-o'-War.

January 1909, p. 185

Fitz criticises Cardinal Logue, Dublin Archbishop Walsh and their brother bishops for refusing to allow the Irish language to be a compulsory subject for entrants to the new National University. Trampling on 'national public opinion' with the Union Jack flying overhead, Logue threatens the vulgar little 'Compulsory Irish' boy with the crozier and the birch. The Cardinal fears that an exclusive Irish language policy would deter 'the quality' from enrolling in the new college. The caption quotes a stinging attack by *Sinn Féin* on the hierarchy's stance

"THAT LITTLE VULGAR BOY."

CARDINAL LOGUE—"Go away, boy. Do you want to ruin my University? This is only a place for gentlemen's sons, and if I let you in I would be boycotted by the 'quality,' so I would."

DR. WALSH—"Sorry for you, my boy, but as I am Chancellor I can't say a word."

[" It is quite possible that in existing circumstances compulsion, instead of being a help, would be a hindrance, to the language movement. It certainly would drive away from the University not a few students."—*Extract from Resolution of the Episcopal Standing Committee, at University College, Stephen's Green, Dublin.*

"The Statement recently published by the Irish Bishops, through their Standing Committee, is in sober truth a dagger aimed at the heart of the Irish nation. . . . . In the coming time, when they look back over the ruin they have wrought, never, never will it lie with them to say, ' An enemy hath done this.' "—" *Sinn Fein*" on "*The Irish Bishops and an Irish University.*"

"There is not an Irishman throughout the whole civilised globe who will not read with feelings of the keenest pain and humiliation the report of the proceedings of the Standing Committee of the Irish Catholic Bishops."—*Letter from Mr. T. O'Donnell, M.P., to "The Irish Independent."*]

That vulgar little boy.
February 1909, p. 197

The treatment of 'pauper burials' at Glasnevin Cemetery aroused public anger in 1906-1909. High charges for even the simplest interment and the use of common burial pits are attacked in this cartoon. The Municipal Council could not intervene directly as Glasnevin Cemeteries Committee was an independent trust, so the Dublin poor are shown here as a bereaved man with his hands tied, while his wife weeps over their child's coffin. The cemetery is shown as greedy Shylock demanding his pound of flesh. Using Shylock to make his point shows that Fitz's readers were familiar with Shakespeare's plays. The caption reports the efforts of a deputation, which included nationalist and suffrage campaigner Jennie Wyse-Power, Labour and Sinn Féin activist P.T. Daly and others, to the City Council to resolve the issue.

THE GLASNEVIN SHYLOCK, OR THE POUND OF FLESH.

PORTIA—"Can no prayers pierce thee? for thy desires are wolfish, bloody, starved and ravenous."
SHYLOCK—"No, none that thou hast wit enough to make; till thou canst rail the seal from off my bond thou but offend'st thy lungs to speak so loud."—*Merchant of Venice, Act iv., Scene 1.*

On the 9th August a monthly meeting of the Municipal Council of the City of Dublin was held in the Mansion House. At twenty minutes past one o'clock the chair was taken by the Right Hon. the Lord Mayor. A deputation on the subject of the Glasnevin Cemetery, consisting of Mr. William Field, M.P., Mrs. Wyse Power, Messrs. P. T. Daly, J. Simmons, and W. Richardson, was received by the Council

Mrs. J. Wyse Power said she appeared to plead for the poor, and in the interests of public decency. That the respect due to the dead was not observed by the authorities of the Glasnevin Cemetery they knew. The shocking facts that had come to light were indisputable. They appealed to the Council to act up to their responsibilities. The method of burying the dead in a fosse or common pit was repugnant to all Christian ideas. Their pagan ancestors would not allow it.

Mr. P. T. Daly said the charges put on the poor in Glasnevin Cemetery were a disgrace to humanity, and the alleged answer of the Secretary was so baseless that it was practically unnecessary to deal with it at any length. The Committee made an average annual profit of £3,500, and surely with that profit they could reduce their charges.

The Glasnevin Shylock, or the pound of flesh.

September 1909, p. 81

The annual Dublin Horse Show was a major feature on the city's social and commercial calendar. *The Lepracaun* produced special Horse Show editions such as this from 1909. A fashionable young lady sits rather precariously on the back of a pleased and prancing centaur. With 'L.S.D' for pounds, shillings and pence, across his waistcoat the centaur is an excellent depiction of the wealthy and rakish 'horsey type' attracted to the city every summer. The portico of the Viceregal Lodge (Áras an Uachtaráin) in the background suggests the elite social whirl of Horse Show Week.

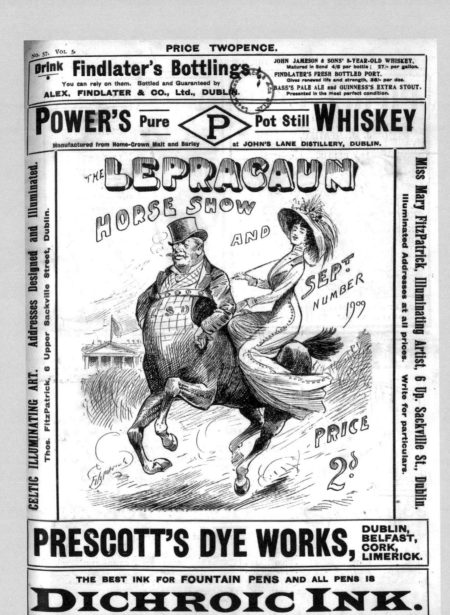

Horse Show issue cover.
September 1909, p. 65

Student 'digs' have long been cause for complaint from both tenants and landladies. Here we see a medical student up from the country, behind in his rent and inflicting considerable 'wear and tear' on the furnishings. His studies seem focused on the sports pages rather than medical textbooks. Through the artwork on the walls Fitz sketches out the middle-class rural family, a simple farm cottage (complete with pig) has somehow produced enough money to put one son through medical school and his brother through the seminary. The fashionable daughter of the house is apparently on the marriage market. The landlady's hopes of payment from this crafty country clan seem pretty low.

THE MEDICAL: "I told you, Mrs. Blinks, I would settle the bill when I hear from my people in the country."
THE LANDLADY: "Your people in the country, bedad; I'll be up in Glasnevin before then."

The medical student.
December 1909, p. 121

Tourism was emerging as a profitable business in Ireland in the early twentieth century, but not all tourists were equally welcome. This 1910 cartoon accompanied a report on a meeting of the Hotels and Tourist Association of Ireland, at which voracious Americans were described as 'the most detestable class of visitors'. *The Lepracaun* agrees with this view of American dining habits, expressing surprise 'that the hotel was not eaten up as well as the menu'. Fitz presents a giant American eagle, complete with star-spangled waistcoat and big cigar, striding after the terrified hotel owner with a hungry eye.

The Annual Meeting of the Hotels and Tourist Association of Ireland was held recently at 190 Great Brunswick Street.

Mr. H. D. Jury, referring to the forthcoming pilgrimage from America, said it was not going to be so large as at first expected, but it would be one of very considerable proportions, and the pilgrimage might become an annual one.

Mr. A. McCleary said that in his experience of American visitors to Irish Hotels they were the most detestable class of visitors to such establishments. He could hardly bring himself to be civil to some of them. He had been in a good many hotels, and very few hotel-keepers whom he had met have a good word to say for their American visitors.

We agree with Mr. McCleary in his remarks, and from our small experience and observation it surprises us that the Hotel was not eaten up as well as the menu. John Bull is only in the halfpenny place.

The American tourist on a whistle-stop tour of Britain and Ireland is captured – almost – in this clever SHY cartoon from 1913.

While we're on the high gear—The latest scheme of

SNAPSHOT OF TOURIST
FROM AMERICA.

hustling American tourists is to "do" the British Isles in a week.

First Tourist—"This is Dublin. Fine city?"
Second Tourist—"Yes; 'twas."
F. T.—"Ah! here we are—Cork."

Dublin was notorious for its overcrowded tenements, one of the worst areas being the 'Monto' around Montgomery Street (now Foley Street), Mountjoy Square and Gardiner Street, shown in this cartoon. In 1911 the Royal Institute of Public Health held its annual congress Dublin with housing problems as a central theme. *The Lepracaun* regularly criticised the city's inability to solve the slum problem, blaming inefficient inspection and enforcement, lack of political will and plain corruption. Many elected members of the Municipal Council were themselves slum-landlords, and so were unlikely to reform the regulations or bring prosecutions. The crocodile, known for his false tears, is a perfect symbol for those public and private commentators who called for something to be done, while living on the rents of the poorest families in the city.

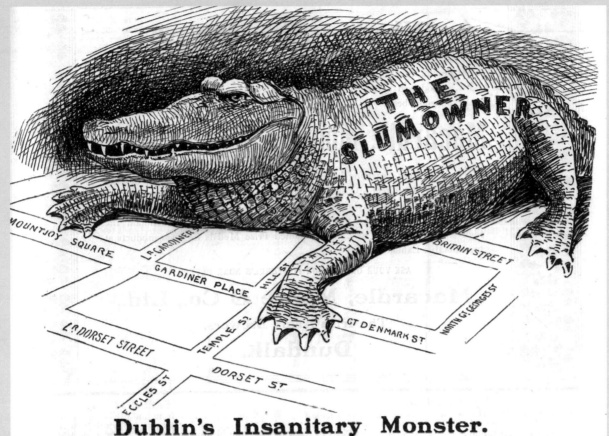

Labels on illustration: MOUNTJOY SQUARE · L{R.GARDINER · GARDINER PLACE · HILL ST · BRITAIN STREET · L{R.DORSET STREET · TEMPLE S? · GT DENMARK ST · NORTH GT GEORGES ST · ECCLES ST · DORSET ST · THE SLUMOWNER

Dublin's Insanitary Monster.

The Congress of the Royal Institute of Public Health, which opens in Dublin on August 15, includes in its programme a series of papers on the Housing Problem. It is to be hoped that a visit to the Dublin slums—largely the property of members of the Dublin Corporation, who weep crocodile tears over the lot of the poor while they are robbing them—will not be omitted.

God sends his creatures light and air
And water open to the skies.
Man locks him in a stifling lair
And wonders why his brother dies.

Dublin's insanitary monster.
August 1911, p. 209

Lloyd George's National Insurance Act, 1911, introduced workers' health insurance paid for by contributions from the state, the employee and -significantly - from the employer. Thousands of people, particularly women, worked in domestic service so every lady's-maid and cook would now cost their employer more. SPEX satirises employers' attempts to avoid paying the contribution by describing their maids as 'companions' or 'guests', rather than staff. However, Mary Ann, the unexpectedly elevated maid, is not impressed this new 'friendship' and would much rather have the health insurance. SPEX draws the employers as lords and ladies when, in fact, many very ordinary middle-income families employed domestic servants.

THE APOTHEOSIS OF MARY ANN.

MARY ANN: "I don't want any of yer sudden compliments at all. Just call me what ye did before—a maid-of-all-work, an' if I'm sick let me get Mr. George's benefit and not be behouldin' to you for it."

[As a result of the Insurance Bill a number of mistresses propose to call their servants "companions" and "guests," in order to avoid coming under its provisions.]

The apotheosis of Mary Ann.

December 1911, p. 253

In April 1912 Vivian Hewitt landed a Blériot monoplane at the Fifteen Acres in the Phoenix Park, having completed the first aerial crossing of the Irish Sea. A fascinated public read how he found his way up the Wicklow coastline and across the city without a detailed map. This three-part cartoon by SHY shows the brave aviator recognising Dublin from the stink of the River Liffey and encountering turbulence in the hot air rising from the politicians in City Hall. The city's Chief Medical Officer for Health, Sir Charles Cameron, urged the public to stop the spread of diseases by catching and killing flies. In the third image Cameron wonders if he should catch this unusual type of fly with his net and paper bag.

THE CHANNEL AND HEWITT WHO FLEW-IT(T).

Viva to you, Hewitt,
You said you would do it.
The Channel you flew it,
   And gave us a thrill.

When you took the notion
Of crossing the ocean
By aerial motion
   To Dublin from Rhyl.

The Channel was breezy,
But you found it easy,
And didn't feel sneezy
   Till you reached our town.
When (so said the papers)
Mysterious vapours
Set you cutting capers
   That near brought you down.

You were lost for a jiffy,
The air became sniffy,
You murmured "The Liffey!
   I'm right"; and you were.

But again you were puzzled,
And felt semi-guzzled,
As retorts semi-muzzled
   Reached you in the air.

Says you, "Now, I wonder
If that could be thunder
They're having down under—
   What is it at all?"

Then came exclamations,
With choice variations;
No more explanations—
   Cork Hill City Hall.

Empty pockets of air, too,
You stated were there, too;
Empty pockets I'll swear, too,
   You'll find in this town.

Though bankruptcy nigher,
The rates, like a flyer,
Keep on mounting higher,
   But seldom come down.

M. P. B.

The Channel and Hewitt who flew-it(t).

May 1912, p. 5

You were lost for a jiffy,
The air became sniffy,
You murmured "The Liffey!
   I'm right"; and you were.

But again you were puzzled,
And felt semi-guzzled,
As retorts semi-muzzled
   Reached you in the air.

Says you, "Now, I wonder
If that could be thunder
They're having down under—
   What is it at all?"

Dublin pedestrians were regularly accosted by charity collectors, cab-drivers, newspaper boys, shoe-shine boys and beggars seeking donations or business. One charity, the Women's National Health Association, hit on the novel idea (familiar to us today) of sticking a badge on the lapel of every donor, showing that they had already contributed. In this cartoon from 1912 SHY extends the concept to show a mixed bunch of street hawkers scowling at a pedestrian safely covered in labels declaring that he has a morning paper, his boots are clean enough - and No! he does not want oranges.

In Dublin, recently, the W.N.H.A. had a street collection day in aid of their cause. Any persons contributing, no matter how small a sum, were presented with a blue star which, being worn by the recipients, indicated that they were not to be called on for any further contribution. A busy city friend of ours who was, like the average pedestrian, the unhappy victim of our numerous army of street vendors, mendicants, etc., has hit upon an idea of developing the Blue Star Label. Above sketch shows what he will appear like some morning.

May 1912, p. 11

In 1912 in Philadelphia a touring cast from the Abbey Theatre were arrested for performing J.M. Synge's 'The Playboy of the Western World' – allegedly an 'immoral or indecent' play. Although the case was dismissed, back in Dublin the public were concerned about the subject matter of some Abbey plays. In a clever exchange between two figures wearing goggles and microbe-proof suits SHY links this moral anxiety to the contemporary concerns about hygiene and disease.

WILL IT COME TO THIS?

FIRST Goggled and otherwise filth=microbe=proofed individual (delving in the dust-bin)—"Eh! where are you going? Go and get a bin for yourself."

SECOND Goggled, etc.—"What are you talking about? I'm a dramatic critic going to the Abbey. Who and what are you?"

FIRST Goggled, etc.—"Oh, I'm an Abbey author looking for the materials of a new play!"

[Last week at the Abbey Theatre a play called "The Magnanimous Lover" was produced, which, according to some critics, left the "Playboy" and "Blanco Posnet" at the post for language and filth. One critic wondered what brought him there, as he was not a Sanitary Inspector].

Will it come to this?
October 1912, p. 68

This was a period of rapid technological innovation, illustrated by the shocked reaction to Germany's huge new airships. SHY has fun with this in four small cartoons; a rifle-wielding airship with the German Kaiser's face threatens an anxious John Bull, representing England; a suffragette airship drops 'Votes for Women' leaflets on a startled male golfer; a Home Rule airship drops 'good wishes' onto a fleeing Orangeman and finally an employer says of a tattered airship wearing Jim Larkin's hat and labelled 'Strike Leader' - 'In Dublin we have a balloon / With ambitions as high as the moon / It's a patched up affair/ Full of bad gas and air / 'Twill burst, we believe, very soon.'

THE SCARESHIPS.

Did you hear of the latest scare—
Of the ships that fly in the air?
   "Why, look," says John Bull,
   "The sky it is full—
They are spying on me, which ain't fair."

Over the golfing green
A hovering airship is seen,
   On destruction intent.
   Hear the golfing gent
Asking her "What does she mean?"

A young man who worked in Belfast
Was seen gazing skywards aghast.
   He then let a yell,
   Which sounded like—well,
"No Surrender" 's a thing of the past.

In Dublin we have a balloon,
With ambitions as high as the moon;
   It's a patched-up affair,
   Full of bad gas and air—
'Twill burst, we believe, very soon.

The scareships.
March 1913, p. 131

A Tango craze swept across the Atlantic in 1913-1914, and with it some stiff clerical condemnation. The cartoon plays on the Dublin Lockout of 1913 and also on a popular painting by Anna Lea Merritt 'Love Locked Out' (1890) which depicts a mournful Cupid pushing at the door of a mausoleum. New York's Cardinal Farley urged Catholics to avoid the Tango (his censure included other dances such as the Turkey Trot and the Bunny Hug) while an Italian cardinal warned against 'a certain dance of transatlantic origin, immoral both in name and character'. The public, however, loved the new dance and SHY clearly shows which side he is on as two sour faces peer out at a rebuked and distraught – but fabulously dressed – dancer.

Another lock-out, or Tango T.T.'s.

January 1914, p. 257

City Politics

Miss Dublin and the Lepracaun give a thorough spring clean to City Hall, labelled 'City Haul' to show how corrupt the editor felt the Municipal Council had become. Among the 'rubbish' being swept out are salaries and increases for city officials, budget over-runs in the new electric lighting system and main drainage improvements, and councillors' entertainment expenses. Dismissing the novelty of workers' representatives the Lepracaun also sweeps away the new Labour councillors. The caption looks forward to a parliament returning to the 'Ould House' on College Green, calling on Irish politicians to prove that they are ready for Home Rule by showing that they are fit to run the city.

WANTED—A CLEAN SWEEP.

The Lepracaun—"I THINK, MISS DUBLIN, BEFORE WE GET THE 'OULD HOUSE' IN COLLEGE GREEN TO DO THE BUSINESS OF THE COUNTRY IN, IT WOULD BE NO HARM TO LET THE NEIGHBOURS SEE WE ARE ABLE TO MAKE A SUCCESS OF THIS ONE FIRST. SO HURRY UP, AND DON'T STOP UNTIL EVERY VESTIGE OF THAT RUBBISH HAS DISAPPEARED."

Wanted – a clean sweep.
May 1905, p. 13

In August 1907 it emerged that, since the time of Charles II (1660-1685), the Lord Mayor of Dublin held the military rank of a 'captain of foot' for which he received an annual salary of £300 from the army.[127] A major Home Rule meeting was due to take place in City Hall the following month, so Fitz shows the mild-mannered Lord Mayor 'Captain' Nannetti leading a rag-tag attack on an anxious John Bull and his British 'Hempire'. A variety of commercial suppliers have lent equipment for the assault while the city's fleet of dredgers, waste disposal ships and turf barges provides naval support. Criticising the ineffective nationalist posturing of the day the cartoonist points out that the pikes, used in 1798 commemorations, are only made of tin. Town Clerk Henry Campbell takes a roll call and Sinn Féin's Thomas Kelly rides in on a donkey wearing a tin helmet and a cork bouyancy jacket.

127 *Irish Times* 14 Aug 1907 p 6.

THE CAPTAIN OF THE CORPORATION FOOT.

In the House of Commons, Aug. 13, Mr. Haldane, Secretary for War, in reply to a question, said, "The Lord Mayor of Dublin receives a perpetual annuity, £300 (Irish), representing the pay of a Captain of Foot."—*Daily Paper.*

Captain of the Corporation Foot.

August 1907, p. 69

The caption quotes a senior judge's condemnation of the terrible living conditons of Dublin's poor. Against a background of disease-ridden and decaying slums (some owned by 'City Fathers' – members of the municipal council) an outraged Miss Dublin accuses the sleeping Public Health Department of presiding over the 'Highest death rate in Europe'. She carries a cat-o-ninetails to whip him into action. The cartoon features many of Dublin's public health challenges; private slaughter-houses still operated within the city; broken drains carried untreated sewage to the slob-lands at Clontarf, unhygenic dairies sold contaminated milk while rubbish and vermin littered the streets in the poorer areas. The risk of contagious diseases such as consumption (T.B), diphtheria and typhoid fever spreading to the rest of the city made middle-class readers anxious for rapid reform. (See also page 107)

Dear, Dirty Dublin. Wanted a Public Health Department.

December 1908, p. 141

Installing the municipal electricity network had gobbled up almost half a million pounds, a vast amount in 1911. Despite the protests of some councillors, the city now proposed to borrow a further £128,000 to complete the project. The caption points out that William Martin Murphy's Dublin United Tram Company had offered to generate the city's electricity for less than a third of the price charged by the municipal network. The cartoon shows a lizard-like mains electrical cable, its mouth crammed with coins, chasing an alarmed middle-class ratepayer across a landscape of 'bad management', 'waste', 'jobbery' etc.

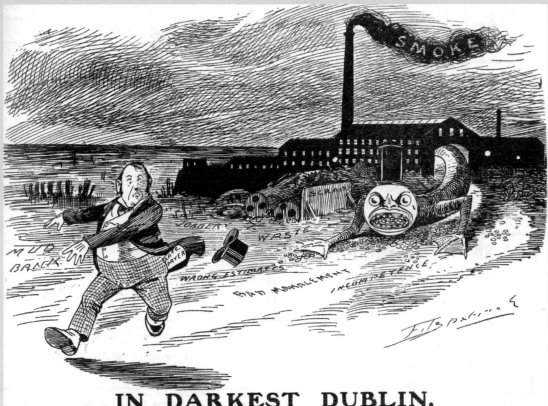

IN DARKEST DUBLIN.

The Dublin Corporation Electricity Committee have issued a report recommending the Council to borrow £128,129 for further extensions to the electricity undertaking. (The report states that net deficit on the undertaking up to 1910 is £14,145.) The original cost of the installation was £590,000.

"I do not think the Corporation is in such good odour with the public as to justify it in applying for over £125,000, . . . especially as the public are paying £10,000 in rates for losses in the electricity undertaking . . . The Committee had not consulted the City Treasurer before meeting to recommend a further loan . . . . amounting to 2s. 6d. in the £ on the City valuation."—*Interview with Ald. Dr. M'Walter, "Irish Independent," January 31, 1911.*

The Dublin United Tram Company some years ago offered to supply the city with electricity—the Corporation using their own mains—at three-farthings per unit. The Corporation charge at present is something like threepence per unit.

The ratepayers appear to have a warm time in store for them.

In darkest Dublin.

February 1911, p. 131

Fitzpatrick uses the story of the Fox and the Grapes from *Aesop's Fables* to satirise the behaviour of Lord Mayor John J. Farrell. In the fable, a fox tries to eat some sweet grapes but cannot reach them, disappointed he says that the grapes were sour and he did not want them anyway. The moral of the tale is that a fool will despise what he cannot achieve. At the same time George V was due to visit the city and a bitter dispute arose over whether the council should give him an official welcome. The king had recently removed anti-Catholic elements from the coronation oath, earning him much praise among Irish nationalists. The cartoon ties the two stories together as the Lord Mayor, having failed to get an increase in his ample salary, announces that even without council approval he will greet the king as an individual Catholic citizen. The regular use of *Aesop's Fables*, Shakespearian plays and classical references shows that *The Lepracaun's* educated readership was familiar with these texts and stories.

Within the past six months four unsuccessful attempts have been made by members of the Dublin Corporation to increase the Lord Mayor's salary by £2,000. Once the motion was carried by a majority of one vote, only to be rescinded a week later, once the resolution was ruled out of order, and the third time it was defeated by a vote of the Council. On the fourth occasion, on June 30, the motion was def-ated by 33 votes to 26. *The Irish Independent*, of July 3, says that his Lordship, on the previous day, declared with emphasis that "if an address is refused to his Majesty by the Corporation of Dublin I will go out myself and welcome the King and thank him as a Catholic for the part he took in having words offensive to my religion deleted from the Coronation Oath."

The fox and the grapes.
July 1911, p. 199

Here the cartoonist S.H.Y (Frank Reynolds) shows Sinn Féin Alderman Thomas Kelly, a staunch campaigner for improved working-class housing in the city. With the collapse of dilapidated tenements on Church Street in 1913 Dublin's chronic housing problem had become more urgent. Demolishing slums left families homeless, building sites in the city centre were expensive but workers could not afford the commute to the distant suburbs – imaginative solutions were called for. SHY unwittingly predicts the future with this satirical illustration of a highrise tower block. In the 1960s Dublin would build a number of such developments. (See also page 105)

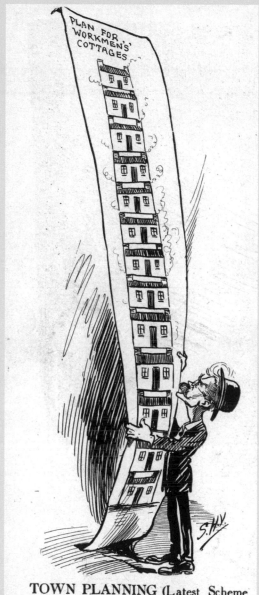

TOWN PLANNING (Latest Scheme

MOTTO—" EXCELSIOR!"

Certainly! Abolish the tenements. Each family a cottage. Suburbs being too far for workers, central ground rent too dear, there being no charge for sky space, the higher the air the purer, we'll build the cottages on top of each other.

Town planning (latest scheme).
July 1914, p. 30

Municipal elections were held each January with the newly-elected councillors attending meetings in their formal civic robes. In this light-hearted cartoon from February 1915 GM (George Monks) shows a procession of little councillors, looking rather pleased with themselves, heading for City Hall. The caption, in the form of a children's rhyme, hopes that this time they might manage to cut the local taxes. The naive innocence of the piece shows how unlikely a hope that is.

See how they go, to the City Hall,
Municipal Councillors, newly elected men,

Let's hope in the rates they'll make a fall
And bring joy to the citizens who selected 'em.

See how they go, to the City Hall...
January 1915, p. 109

The proposal to build new municipal offices prompted SHY to suggest building a new City Hall on the model of the large gas-storage tanks, or 'gas retorts', which stood at South Lotts Road. Like the real gas tanks, the roof could rise or fall depending on the amount of hot air produced by the councillors. The neat play on words with 'gas retorts' and political retorts sharpens the satire nicely. SHY might have smiled to learn that he had once again predicted the future when the South Lotts gasworks were converted into apartments in 2005.

In 1913 Sir Hugh Lane proposed that a Municipal Gallery of Modern Art be built across the Liffey, replacing the Ha'penny Bridge. The footbridge was unpopular not only because of its toll but also because of the unsightly advertising hoardings attached to it. Many citizens objected to the new gallery proposal and it was finally defeated, largely through the efforts of William Martin Murphy and his *Irish Independent* newspaper. SHY's cartoon refers to a common complaint, that the new gallery would block the view of the sunset upriver. The pun on Sir Hugh's name in the text below the sketch is typical Lepracaun wit.

CITY IMPROVEMENTS.

NEW MUNICIPAL BUILDINGS.

We understand that plans have been submitted for new municipal buildings. If we are not too late, we beg to offer a design which, we think, would be in keeping with the traditions of the present Cork Hill Temple. The idea is this: An edifice built something on the style of our city gas retorts. The roof to be movable, so as to be ready for any strain occasioned by the generating powers of our city representatives, some of whom are famed for their "gas" and others for their retorts. In the background might be placed a cooling tank, to be used during heated debates, while in the foreground a cellar would be required, in which to dump the ratepayers' monies, which would be necessary to keep the municipal pot boiling.

THE NEW ART GALLERY.

The members of the Royal Institute of Architects, Ireland, have decided the "bridge site" is unsuitable for the proposed New Art Gallery. We would suggest that the building in question be erected somewhere along the proposed new street, which is to connect Henry street with Dame street. We could then call the new thoroughfare "Sir Hugh" Lane.

LIGHTING IMPROVEMENTS.

We noticed recently in some of the suburbs that small electric lamps were erected in place of the old gas illuminators. For some reason or other, after a few weeks of electric light, the "Angels of Light" Committee gents suddenly changed their minds, and the suburbs are once more diffused with the soft gas glow. Evidently the Lighting Committee prefer the gas-trick to the electric.

City improvements.
April 1913, p. 140

Lady Ishbel Abderdeen, forceful wife of the Lord Lieutenant, was renowned (and ridiculed) for her campaign to educate the public about tuberculosis (TB). While science was identifying TB as a contagious condition it was still popularly considered a 'constitutional disease' - a natural feature of life feature of life among the poor. Here, Miss Common Sense stands in a similar slum district to that shown in December 1908 (See page 95) when Miss Dublin called for action on public health, but on this occasion the cartoonist dismisses the elegant arictocrat's efforts as nonsense. He believes that starving children are a more urgent concern. It would be some years before the links between poor nutrition, ineffective sanitation, decayed housing and contagious disease would be universally recognised. The gap between the average tenement family's 12 shillings and 9 pence per week, and the Lord Lieutenant's £22,000 annual salary (around €2,500,000 today), is highlighted in the scroll carried by carried by Lady Aberdeen. The fact that her information leaflets were printed in London while Dublin printers were desperate for business was a further mark against her in the cartoonists' opinion.

Common Sense and Nonsense.

An exhibition in connection with the campaign against consumption in this country was opened in the Town Hall, Rathmines, by her Excellency the Countess of Aberdeen.

LADY ABERDEEN—"Just as I was leaving the Vice-regal Lodge, I received a letter from Sir Robert Matheson, Registrar-General, with the good tidings that all forms of tubercular disease is down **one decimal point**. Is it not splendid?"

COMMON SENSE—"I don't see the point, your Excellency. All I can say is that there are thousands of children starving in our city, getting nothing to eat except what they beg. If you tried to do something for the little ones, it would be more charitable and practical than holding exhibitions and wasting money on your travelling circus."

Common sense and nonsense.
June 1909, p. 30

National Politics

Fitz regularly used 'Pat' the common-sense, respectable Irishman (as opposed to the derogatory 'Paddy' character presented in *Punch* and other British periodicals) to represent moderate public opinion in Ireland. Most nationalists supported the Irish Parliamentary Party, recently reunified under John Redmond after a bitter split. Here we see Pat at the start of 1907, sinking into a quagmire of competing political parties. The ghostly banshees, omens of doom, floating about his head are the 'Nationalists Party' who seek Home Rule; the unionist 'Orange party' who want to remain within the United Kingdom; the 'Gaelic Party' is the rising new Irish-Ireland movement which included Sinn Féin and a variety of Gaelic cultural organisations such as the Gaelic League. The 'Devolution Party' refers to a short-lived proposal to establish an Irish assembly with fewer powers than a Home Rule parliament. Some nationalist leaders were briefly tempted by this offer but it was rejected by the grass-roots of the Irish Parliamentary Party. This cartoon captures a moment when it was unclear which way Pat would turn.

THE FOUR BANSHEES OF ERIN.

PAT—" Here I am into another year and I am getting deeper
and deeper in the mire."

The four banshees of Erin.
February 1907, p. 421

As a committed constitutional politician John Redmond was opposed to armed revolt, however the welcome offered in 1907 to General Louis Botha, first Prime Minister of the Transvaal in South Africa, must have given him some pause for thought. Botha, leader of the rebellious Boers in the recent war against the British Empire, is shown here with a noble martial bearing carrying a rifle and wearing a sword, having arrived in England on the Royal Mail steamer *Carisbrook Castle*. The Transvaal had achieved self-government within the empire, the goal which had eluded Ireland for a century. A portly Redmond, with his primitive stick labelled 'constitutional agitation' under his arm, watches gloomily – even Botha's luggage is smarter than Redmond's peasant bundle. The grovelling John Bull, Fitz's unflattering representation of England, polishes Botha's boots and remembers the crippling cost of the South African War. Perhaps Redmond is speaking for more radical nationalists when he observes that Botha's military 'accoutrements' made all the difference.

"ON THE KNEE."

JOHNNY BULL (reading address)—'' My dear General, this is one of the proudest moments of my ————.''
JOHN REDMOND (in the shade)—'' I wonder when will my turn come. I see the Accoutrements have done the trick.''

[General Louis Botha, first Prime Minister of the Transvaal, has arrived in England, and Southampton, which saw so many troops off to meet the new Premier's troops in battle only a few years ago, welcomed him now with all honours. The Mayor and Corporation assembled in state, and offered the General a sincere and hearty welcome on landing from the Carisbrook Castle.]

On the knee.
May 1905, p. 9

113

Miss Erin, the eminently respectable personification of Ireland, is deafened by the competing efforts of the old Irish Party barrel organ and its new Sinn Féin competitor; she urges them both to play the same tune. Sinn Féin's 'blind' organ-grinder is Sir Thomas Grattan Esmonde, former Irish Parliamentary Party MP for North Wexford, who switched to the new party in 1907. Fitz presents him as having been blind to the IPP's failings for many years. Beside Esmonde's music box, with its pun on Sinn Féin ('We Ourselves') and an unreliable sunburst of freedom, stands the Sinn Féin Irish terrier wearing a collection-box on its collar. Redmond, accompanied by the party monkey the *Freeman's Journal*, grinds the IPP barrel-organ emblazoned with the old parliament house on College Green and the royal monogram 'G.R.' beneath a crown. Miss Erin is clearly not going to fund either of their efforts this time.

THE RIVAL HURDY-GURDYS.

MISS ERIN.—"Go away, please, gentlemen; this noise is awful. If you expect me to pay you for discord, you're quite mistaken. When you've practised a little harmony you can call round again."

The rival hurdy-gurdys.
August 1907, p. 75

In legend, the Old Man of The Sea would trick travellers into carrying him across a stream but would then refuse to let them go, forcing the unfortunate dupe to carry him wherever he directed. This 1907 cartoon suggests that Redmond and the Irish Parliamentary Party are being tricked into carrying a rather sinister looking Sinn Féin across the dangerous waters of parliamentary politics, implying that Sinn Féin will set the political agenda in the future. The caption quotes Sir Thomas Esmonde MP, as he abandons the IPP's parliamentary policy and joins Sinn Féin's more radical campaign. (See also In the Bog on page 163)

THE NEW "OLD MAN OF THE SEA."

"I am convinced that Parliamentary agitation, as now conducted, has spent its force, and that nothing more can be gained by it on its present lines." . . . . . "I do not believe that the English-speaking people will ever grant Home Rule or anything like it."

Letter from SIR THOMAS ESMONDE, M.P.—*Daily Papers*, July 22nd, 1907.

The new 'Old Man of the Sea'.
August 1907, p. 57

Reflecting both the new politics and new technology, Fitz shows Redmond as an old-fashioned jarvey driving a traditional Irish side-car labelled 'parliamentarianism'. Observing the new Sinn Féin automobile speeding away in a different direction, Redmond's comment shows a concern about competition for political funds. The Sinn Féin label is always written in Gaelic script (which Redmond describes as 'foreign'), presenting it as more 'Irish' than the older Irish Parliamentary Party. Anxiety was acute among IPP supporters about the Sinn Féin threat, as no opponent had ever disputed the IPP's claim to represent the will of Irish nationalism. However, the party would regain its prominent position in the period up to 1914.

A THING OF THE PAST.

JOHN REDMOND—"Bad luck to that infernal machine with the foreign name. Ever since it come on the road I have lost any fares I had. I can't afford to give the poor baste a feed of oats. I'm to blame meself. Me ould yoke is a bit slow, and it's out of date. I was wan time in comfortable circumstances."

A thing of the past.
September 1907, p. 97

In October 1907 Lord Dunraven, a moderate Unionist, called for a return to the spirit of his 'Conciliation Conference' of 1902 which had produced such positive results in reforming land ownership, but his appeal fell on deaf ears. Inspired by the Christmas spirit, this cartoon from December 1907 shows a somewhat battered Angel of Peace despairing of Ireland's political factions. Amidst cries of 'unity' rival supporters of Timothy Healy, William O'Brien, John Dillon and John Redmond vie with each other and with members of the Gaelic League, the Ancient Order of Hibernians, Sinn Féin, the Orange Order and supporters of the Irish Council (Devolution) proposals. Labour and the trade union movement are not shown, possibly because Fitz assumed they were represented within the range of nationalist factions.

THE CALL FOR UNITY.

THE ANGEL.—"Bedad, it's meself that's tired of coming out and trying to separate them, fighting like divils for Conciliation, and hatin' aich other for the pure love of God."

The call for unity.
December 1907, p. 143

In this 'before and after' cartoon Dublin municipal councillor Seán T. O'Kelly, alderman Thomas Kelly and Arthur Griffith, editor of the *Sinn Féin* newspaper, take the Sinn Féin mastiff to a dog-fight – the North Leitrim by-election. The dog, or candidate, is Charles J. Dolan a former Irish Parliamentary Party MP for the constituency who resigned his seat after converting to Sinn Fein's abstentionist policy. Following a bitter and often violent campaign he was beaten by local county councillor Francis Meehan. Despite losing the election, the new party gained much support nationally for its stance. In the 'before' scene Dolan is spoiling for a fight, but after the contest he is returned to Dublin in a wheelbarrow carrying the Dublin Corporation crest. At this time Sinn Féin were calling for all official signs, on municipal vehicles and equipment, to be printed in Irish.

A sure thing – All broke up.
March 1908, p. 213

Fair-ground showmen John Redmond and John Dillon of the Irish Parliamentary Party try to trick sensible Pat out of his money - but he is not fooled. Fitz's cartoon neatly illustrates the attitude of many nationalists who were growing sceptical of Redmond's endless promises of Home Rule. In self-assured tones the showman dismisses Pat's doubts while insisting on his money. The Irish in America, a vital souce of political funds, had apparently been taken in by Redmond's assurances on his recent visit. The pun on the sentimental Irish-American tune 'Come back to Erin' is nicely pointed.

"HOME RULE IS IN SIGHT."
THE PARLIAMENTARY PEEP-SHOW.

MR. REDMOND : "This picture is called 'Home Rule in Sight.' It created quite a sensation in the States on the occasion of my last visit."

PAT : "I can't see any Home Rule."

MR. REDMOND : "Well, my boy, your vision must be a trifle bad. I guess you have seen enough for what you paid. You pay your money, and don't ask silly questions. I've said it's there, and that's all right."

The orchestra plays "Come Back to Earn."

[Mr. Redmond has assured a meeting in Boston that "Home Rule was in sight." It is a pity Mr. Redmond did not enter into details, and state at what exact point of the horizon Home Rule could be seen, and from whom we are to get it.]

'Home Rule is in sight.' The parliamentary peep-show.

November 1908, p. 125

In January 1910 the Liberal party came to power in Westminster in a landslide victory. In a satirical, if slightly optimistic, cartoon we see newly-elected Prime Minister Herbert Asquith holding up the Unionist Party traffic to allow Irish Parliamentary Party nursemaids John Dillon and T.P. (Tay Pay) O'Connor to push the Home Rule baby across the road. Some doubt as to the eventual outcome is expressed by the fact that the baby, played by a diminutive John Redmond, is being fed on Liberal promises and the label on the pram has rebranded the party as the 'Irish (Liberal) Party'. Constable Asquith appears again in January 1911 when Home Rule seemed somewhat more achievable (perhaps). (See also Softsoap First! page 133)

HIS MAJESTY THE PARLIAMENTARY BABY.

His Majesty the parliamentary baby.
February 1910, p. 179

Miss Erin attempts to stop a prosperous looking John Redmond from heading on a fund-raising trip to America and Canada while the nationalist movement disintegrates into faction fighting on the quayside. The Cork nationalist MP William O'Brien had founded a new 'All for Ireland League' in March 1910 and the caption quotes his criticisms of Redmond's mission to America. Fitz shows the United Irish League (UIL), the constituency organisation for the Irish Parliamentary Party, and Redmond's deputy John Dillon squaring up to ardent anti-Redmondite Timothy Healy, who drags his coat on the ground in the traditional faction-fighter's invitation 'who'll dare to step on my coat tails'. The chaos makes Redmond's desire to go abroad seem more understandable!

A Collection for a Deserving Charity.

ERIN—"Stop ; where are you off to ?"

MR. REDMOND—"To America, to collect money for the Cause."

ERIN—"The Cause ! Is it to keep up this miserable faction, and to make me the laughing-stock of the world."

Messrs. John Redmond, Joseph Devlin, T. P. O'Connor, and Alderman Daniel Boyle left Queenstown recently on board the Baltic for a tour in America and Canada to raise funds for the Irish National cause.

"We have gone often before to tell our countrymen there that although the sky was dark and we could not see the breaking of the dawn, that still the old fight was up in Ireland, and we asked them to hold up their hands and to give us their moral and material assistance ; but to-day I go to America under far different circumstances."—*Mr. John Redmond, at Queenstown, September 17th, 1910.*

"All that stuff of Mr. Redmond's was simply manufactured for export to America. There is not a man in the House of Commons, and least of all Mr. Redmond, who believes one word of what he tells you about the cataclysm that is about to overtake the House of Lords."—*Mr. William O'Brien, at Dungarvan, September 18th, 1910.*

"As to being on the eve of Home Rule, so they were, but it was Tib's Eve (at which there was laughter). . . . . He deliberately said that so long as the present methods of the Irish Party were persisted in they were farther from any practical possibility of Home Rule from England than they were 25 years ago (hear, hear)."—*Mr. William O'Brien, at Kilmallock, September 10th, 1910.*

A collection for a deserving charity.

October 1910, p. 71

This cartoon comes from the second General Election of 1910, when both British political parties, depicted as old-fashioned country gents, tried to woo the Irish electorate. An exasperated and unconvinced Miss Erin dismisses both Squire Asquith's Liberal gift of Home Rule ('Tay Pay' is a reference to leading Irish Parliamentary Party member T.P. O'Connor) and Squire Campbell-Bannerman's Conservative policy of Irish devolution. In a possible nod to Sinn Féin's position she declares that she will go her own way, the use of Gaelic script on her skirt seems to support this. The 18th century English writer Dr. Johnson described patriotism as 'the last refuge of the scoundrel'.

How Happy Could She be with Neither.

"Arrah, don't be moidherin' me with your 'where are ye goin', my pretty maid?' I'm goin' me own way; an' let me tell you both that me opinion of the pair o' yer politics is what Docthor Johnson said was 'the last refuge of a scoundrel.'"

How happy could she be with neither.
December 1910, p. 99

In January 1911 the unpredictable nature of electoral politics left the Irish Parliamentary Party holding the balance of power in Westminster. At last, or so it seemed, Redmond's moment had come. In this particularly sharp cartoon Fitz plays on a famous advertisement for Sunlight Soap drawing the Liberal Prime Minister Asquith as a traffic policeman holding back two great forces in British politics, the House of Lords and the Women's Suffrage campaign, to allow a delightfully prim John Redmond to carry his Home Rule parcel safely across. The label 'Soft Soap' on both the parcel and the cartoon show that the Irish public were not fully convinced. (See also His Majesty the parliamentary baby, page 127)

Sunlight First! c. 1910

Softsoap First!

January 1911, p. 128

In July 1911 King George V and Queen Mary made a royal visit to Ireland. While some radical socialists and nationalists protested against the trip the dawning possibility of Home Rule, and the king's decision to visit the Catholic seminary at Maynooth, helped ensure a generally positive reception. Fitz presents his readers with a respectful depiction of the monarch addressing Pat, the 'average Irishman', in friendly terms. Pat gives a warm welcome but it is conditional, moderate nationalism is polite and patient – but not forever. Standing in front of the old parliament house on College Green he reminds the king that next time he should bring Home Rule, which his government (not the king himself) has promised. The Union Jack is noticeably absent from the flags fluttering overhead.

A FLYING VISIT.

HIS MAJESTY—"Just dropped in, Pat, to see how you are going on."

PAT—"Welcome, your Majesty; I could be a lot worse, but I'm looking forward to that little Parliament your Government has promised me so long, and I hope you'll bring it on your next visit."

A flying visit.
July 1911, p. 195

In September 1911, as Home Rule draws closer, Erin yearns for its arrival, but many former hopes have been smashed on the rocks. The wreckage of earlier Irish rebellions, Wolfe Tone's attempt in 1798, Young Ireland in 1848 and the Fenian Rising of 1865, emphasise the tension in the caption. More commonly heard as 'There's many a slip 'twixt cup and lip' or 'Don't count your chickens until they're hatched', the moral is the same - politics is an unpredictable business. Behind the eagerly awaited ship is the traditional 'sunburst' of freedom, an emblem appearing in nationalist cartoons and republican flags to the present day.

EXPECTANCY.

There's many a slip 'twixt
The shore and the ship.

Expectancy.
September 1911, p. 219

Miss Erin sits by her traditional cottage fireside in this SPEX cartoon from Christmas 1911. The image might be either sad or hopeful – is the smoke of 'neglect' and 'emigration' obscuring Home Rule, or does the promise of self-government shine through the gloom? The caption echoes these mixed emotions, felt so keenly at Christmas time. The lines are from Alfred, Lord Tennyson's *In Memoriam* a lengthy poetic lament for a close friend who died young. Many of *The Lepracaun's* readers would know the poem, and the stanzas from which these two lines are taken. It seemed that Home Rule had arrived just in time, Irish nationalists were about to abandon all hope: *This year I slept and woke with pain /I almost wish'd no more to wake/And that my hold on life would break/Before I heard those bells again/But they my troubled spirit rule/ For they controll'd me when a boy/They bring me sorrow touch'd with joy/ The merry, merry bells of Yule.* Despite her long, sad history and her current woes this Yuletide Miss Erin has cause for hope.

CHRISTMAS, 1911.

"They bring me sorrow touch'd with joy,
The merry, merry bells of Yule."

Christmas 1911.
December 1911, p. 263

The passage of the Parliament Act of 1911 had finally broken the House of Lords' veto and cleared the way for Irish Home Rule. Here Redmond is in the driving seat taking Ireland, presented as a sovereign queen with her shamrock crown and Home Rule flag, to her destination. Dismissing the vocal opposition of Edward Carson, leader of the Ulster Unionists, Andrew Bonar Law, leader of the Conservative and Unionist Party and fellow party member Lord Londonderry, Redmond describes them as noisy but harmless – now that the House of Lords has been tamed. The Unionists have evidently dined on 'hatred' and 'bigotry' and, unlike the cartoon on page 119, this time Redmond is driving a smart new motor car - he is clearly the man of the moment.

"BOW=WOW=WOW."

ERIN—"John, what is that savage, discordant noise I hear?"
CHAUFFEUR JOHN—"It is only the barking of some vicious dogs; but as they are tied up they can't bite as they should like to do."

Bow-wow-wow.

May 1912, p. 3

In early 1912 Home Rule was growing closer and Ulster unionist resistance was intensifying. Negotiations to woo unionist opinion with improved conditions were unsuccessful. Here Mrs. Erin, in most reasonable terms, invites the unwilling infant with his workers' flat cap and Orange Order drum, to the best seat in the house. The cartoon's title is a clear representation of nationalist attitudes towards Ulster Unionism.

THE SPOILT CHILD.

MRS. ERIN—"Do, like a good child, come in out of the cold; we have kept the best seat at the fire for you."
SPOILT CHILD—"I don't want the best seat; I want the whole fire."

The spoilt child.
May 1912, p. 7

As Unionist resistance to Home Rule stiffened during 1912 nationalists came to see them as unreasonably stubborn. SPEX captures this attitude nicely as Miss Erin tries to coax the petulant boy 'N.E.Ulster' into the 'Home Sweet Home Rule' cottage. The sulking lad wears the cap of a Belfast industrial worker, factory chimneys rise behind him and his drum is burst. The bottle of Boyne Water refers both to the Battle of the Boyne (1690) and to the Orange ballad 'The Boyne Water'. Significantly, the rest of Ulster is already in the cottage garden along with the farmers' sons from Connaught and Munster. Even the scholar from Leinster, a reference to more moderate Southern unionists in Trinity College and Dublin's suburbs, has joined in. The irreconcilable Unionist is presented as an awkward minority. A similarly dismissive nationalist attitude is seen in other *Lepracaun* cartoons, reflecting a widely-held opinion towards Ulster Unionism.

The Irreconcilable.
October 1912, p. 65

As leader of the newly formed Ulster Unionist party (1910) Dubliner Edward Carson was a frequent target for *The Lepracaun*'s cartoonists during the Ulster Crisis (1912-14). Nationalists were amused to see the ultra-loyal Carson portrayed as a traitor to the crown. The split collar sticking out below his firm jaw reminded readers of Carson's senior legal position on the privy council. As leader of the campaign to resist the power of parliament, especially on 'Ulster Day' (28 September 1912) when a quarter of a million Unionist men and women declared their opposition to Home Rule, Carson is presented here as 'King Edward VIII' – sharing the throne with a clearly uncomfortable George V. Armed with a cudgel, King Carson tramples on 'every law of the land', while clouds of 'treason', 'sedition' and 'lies' rumble in the background. The term 'dual monarchy' is a reference to the Austro-Hungarian system of government. Ironically Sinn Féin founder Arthur Griffith suggested such an arrangement for Ireland in his book *The Resurrection of Hungary* (1904). The subtitle 'I and my king' refers to the over-ambitious Cardinal Wolsey (1470-1530) who fell foul of King Henry VIII by using this expression, which places the monarch below his subject. Henry had Wolsey arrested and removed from office. SPEX warns of (or perhaps recommends) a similar outcome for Carson.

A SECOND DUAL MONARCHY.
King Edward VIII.
v.
George the V.
or
I AND MY KING.

A second dual monarchy.
King Edward VIII v. George the V.
or I and my king.
October 1912, p. 69

Nationalists did not take the new Ulster Volunteers very seriously during the summer of 1913. The Volunteer leaders General Sir George Richardson and Captain James Craig had described the new force as being similar to the official Territorials, a reserve force formed in 1908 to support the British Army, hence the clever pun on Derry and Tory here. In this cartoon SHY is obviously unimpressed, as a rag-tag bunch of civilians in ill-fitting uniforms with wooden rifles and other makeshift weapons drop their 'No Surrender' banner and scatter at the arrival of a lone policeman. The situation would change dramatically in April 1914 when the Ulster Volunteers imported thousands of rifles and millions of rounds of ammunition at Larne, Co. Antrim.

THE DERRY TORYALS.

On condition that Home Rule is not passed as an Act of Parliament, **CAPTAIN CRAIG**, we believe, has offered the uses of his Volunteer Ulster Army to England as Territorials. Ah! well can we imagine this sturdy Shankhill soldiery standing in bottle array—(pardon, we meant "battle array, but in the excitement——). Well, as we said before, we can imagine this valiant corps of "last ditchers," this brave wooden gun brigade, this gallant array of Orange pips, awaiting the signal to fight. Well can we imagine the frenzied clash and the terror-inspiring charge of this mighty muster of men when they get the word——

"POLICE"! ! ! !

The Derry Toryals.
August 1913, p. 192

The prevalence of militant activity in Ireland is shown in this somewhat illogical cartoon from the Chrismas 1913 edition. The Irish terrier, symbol of Ireland's fighting spirit, bares his teeth to reveal the Ulster Volunteers, militant Suffragettes, the Irish Citizen Army and the Irish Volunteers. The tiny British bulldog in his Boy Scout's uniform cowers in fright. At no point, however, could the forces of Ulster unionism, nationalism, militant suffragism and radical socialism have combined into a combined Irish 'bite'. Perhaps the cartoon reveals a pride in the self-reliant activism of Irish people – of whichever political hue.

The Irish terrier.
December 1913, p. 241

The three southern provinces respond to the cries of Ulster, trapped on a rock labelled 'N.E. Ulster' and separated by the treacherous waters of 'bigotry' and 'hate'. Carson and fellow Unionist F.E. Smith patrol the coast carrying a flag threatening 'Civil Warrr' in the tones of a stage-villain, but their boat is named 'The Bluff' suggesting that Carson's forces will not carry out their threats. The sunburst of Home Rule pushes back the clouds of doom surrounding isolated Ulster. In 1913-14 Ulster Unionists were negotiating an opt-out from Home Rule, whether this would be for four or six counties, or for the entire province, was a controversial point. SPEX's cartoon emphasises the minority nature of the unionist position by showing Ulster seeking to be rescued from N.E. Ulster – the heartland of opposition to Home Rule. The other provinces' offer to do 'anything' to save their separated sister appears to be limited to political action, there is no threat of force.

MAROONED.

OR IS THIS TO BE ULSTER'S FATE AS DESIGNED BY HER CHAMPIONS, CARSON & CO.?

ULSTER: " Help, help! O, take me back from this wretched place, where I haven't room to stir, and where no one will come near me!"

THE SISTER PROVINCES—" We will do anything, even to battling through this sea of infamy, to bring you back to the dear old main land."

Marooned.
March 1914, p. 279

The Irish Volunteers were formed in November 1913 as a response to the anti-Home Rule Ulster Volunteers. By April 1914 the new nationalist army was feeling more self-confident, as illustrated by this encounter between Pat, a grown man, and the small Ulster boy. *Lepracaun* cartoons repeatedly depict Ulster unionism as a child, suggesting a lack of maturity or understanding and implying that he can be made to behave himself. On this occasion, however, the Ulster lad is smartly dressed and resolute rather than spoilt and petulant. To have 'green in your eye' is to be easily fooled, so Pat clearly does not believe Ulster's threat of civil war. Confusingly, the names 'Irish Volunteers' and 'National Volunteers' are used interchangeably (and sometimes together) in *The Lepracaun*. At the start of the Great War the organisation split into the majority National Volunteers, who supported Redmond's cooperation with the British war effort, and the minority Irish Volunteers who were unwilling to serve in British uniform. This latter group would go on to fight in the Easter Rising of 1916.

APRIL THE FIRST; OR, NO GREEN IN HIS EYE.

PAT (to Young Ulster Volunteer)—"Look here now, young fellow me lad, none of your April fool tricks here, or I might show you a better one."

April the first, or No green in his eye.
April 1914, p. 295

The Home Rule Bill passed successfully through the House of Commons on 25 May 1914, in time for SPEX to produce this neighbourly version of the parliamentary event. A slim and respectable Mrs Erin stands in her own doorway as a rather blousy Mrs Britannia returns the keys. In a friendly exchange the two housewives settle their former differences as Mrs Erin's boys laugh and skip around her. Little Ulster, however, seems far from pleased at the proceedings. Mrs Erin's willingness to 'lend a hand' would be tested when war broke out in August 1914 and tens of thousands of Irish nationalists volunteered for service in British uniform.

RESTITUTION.

MRS. BRITANNIA—"Dear Mrs. Erin, I've just stepped round to return you the keys of your house, and I hope, now that there is no quarrel between us, we shall be good friends."

MRS. ERIN—"My dear Mrs. Britannia, I'm really thankful to you, and trust that we shall be excellent friends for the future and always ready to lend a hand to one another."

Restitution.
June 1914, p. 17

In this cartoon delays over the introduction of Home Rule and obstruction from Ulster Unionism have finally exhausted nationalist patience. The National Volunteer infant has grown strong and sturdy on a diet of 'patriotism'. No longer prepared to be soothed by Liberal promises or 'meaningless rocking', he climbs out of his cot and demands arms. This image was published shortly before the Howth gun-running of 26 July 1914 when the Irish Volunteers imported hundreds of rifles into Dublin. As the arms were being brought to the city an encounter between the British military and a hostile crowd of unarmed onlookers resulted in three civilians being shot dead, a fourth died later of bayonet wounds.

THE "N.V." BABY (not in Arms)!

THE BABY: " Here! I've grown too big for this meaningless rocking. I want arms!

The N.V. Baby (not in arms)!
July 1914, p. 36

It is August 1914 and war has broken out in Europe. For directly opposite strategic reasons John Redmond and Edward Carson pledge their volunteers in support of the British war effort. Perhaps this cartoon suggests a sense of relief as Ireland narrowly avoids civil war between nationalists and unionists. The new war is at a safe distance, the choppy sea separates Ireland from hostilities (or so the cartoonist thought). With a sincere and manly hand-shake the two leaders agree to defend their shared islands from any invader. Within a few weeks, however, thousands of nationalists and unionists would enlist for service overseas, enduring a common fate from the Western Front to the Middle East.

PAX IN BELLUM; or, UNITED KINGDOMERS.

JOHN—"My dear Edward, if you and I ever fight, it will be shoulder to shoulder against any outsider who ventures to attack these islands sacred to both of us."
EDWARD—"My dear old friend, there's my hand on it."

Pax in Bellum, or United Kingdomers.
August 1914, p. 39

In a reprise of the 'New old man of the sea' cartoon from August 1907, Mary Fitzpatrick depicts the split in the Irish Volunteer movement. Following a speech by John Redmond in September 1914 a majority of members supported his call for volunteers to join the British Army in the Great War, these were renamed the National Volunteers. The remainder, who kept the name of Irish Volunteers, rejected the idea of fighting in British uniform. In this drawing the Provisional Committee, dominated by Redmond appointees, is shown as the wily 'Old Man' riding on the shoulders of the volunteer movement and directing where it will go. The poor quality of the drawing, and the recycling of an earlier idea, indicate the difficulties which *The Lepracaun* faced following the death of its founder in 1912 and the challenging business conditions at the start of the war. (See also The new "Old Man of the Sea" on page 117)

IN THE BOG.

"The last office to which I was appointed, and one of the proudest that I occupy, is President of the National Volunteer Organisation."—Mr. John Redmond, at Kilkenny, October, 18.

"Mr. Redmond is no longer entitled, through his nominees, to any place in the administration and guidance of the Irish Volunteer Organisation. . . . We shall propose . . . (4) To repudiate any undertaking, by whomsoever given, to consent to the legislative dismemberment of Ireland, and to protest against the present attitude of the present Government, who, under the pretence that Ulster cannot be coerced, avow themselves prepared to coerce the Nationalists of Ulster."—From the manifesto issued by Professor John MacNeill, Chairman, and nineteen members of the original Volunteer Committee.

In the bog.
October 1914, p. 65

Women

The Lepracaun Cartoon Monthly reflected the conventional social values and assumptions of its respectable middle-class nationalist readers. Here Fitz, the editor and cartoonist-in-chief, satirised the flirting and banter between young Dublin women of a certain class and the many soldiers stationed in the city. A variety of uniforms, from tight waists and tight trousers to kilts and great-coats, attract admiring looks from the civilian females strolling on Sackville Street (O'Connell Street). The young ladies, however, seem a little too forward for the cartoonist's liking. Tyler's Boots and McDowell Jewellers, regular advertisers in *The Lepracaun*, appear in the background along with the offices of the *Daily Independent* and *Evening Herald*. The caption reminds us that this courtship ritual could be observed on the street every Sunday from 3.00pm until the small hours of the morning. Although 'The Monto', Dublin's infamous red-light district, was close by the illustration does not imply a commercial side to these meetings.

"CIVIL AND UNCIVIL SERVANTS."

SACKVILLE STREET—The Finest Thoroughfare in the World—Every Sunday from 3 p.m. to 1 a.m.

We hear with pleasure that the British Army is to be reduced by 20,000 men; it will be a serious loss to Dublin.

Civil and uncivil servants.

August 1908, p. 315

At the start of the twentieth century there were a growing number of employment options for women. The Post Office had opened some junior clerical roles to female applicants, but a woman in the workplace was still something of a novelty. Fitz's cartoon of frivolous female Post Office employees, easily distracted by hats and needlework, probably raised a chuckle among many readers. Interestingly, a lady golfer in a long pale coat is one of the delayed customers crowding around the post-office counter. Perhaps *The Lepracaun*'s female readers in 1906 were less amused, but could they have suspected how long it might take to get full membership of some golf clubs?

SHOULD LADIES BE EMPLOYED IN THE POSTAL SERVICE?
From letters received on the subject, we say certainly yes! if the stamp collectors only had patience.

Should ladies be employed in the postal service?
October 1910, p. 350

This crowded cartoon is a satire of a satire. Gilbert & Sullivan's hugely successful comic opera 'Patience, or Bunthorne's Bride' (1881) lampooned the Aesthetic movement in art and literature. In the opera groups of women swoon around the romantic male lead, a poet of the most aesthetic kind. Linking female fans and women's suffrage Fitz reports on Tom Kettle MP, a young star of the Irish Parliamentary Party, attending a women's suffrage meeting. Kettle promises votes in a Home Rule parliament to adoring women in outlandish hats (which Fitz found endlessly amusing) and to one mannish matron. His poster, however, casts some doubt on this political pledge. In the background the bearded Francis Sheehy-Skeffington, nationalist and feminist in his trademark tweed knickerbockers, sings 'Put Me Among The Girls' a popular song of the era. The lengthy poetic caption is a good parody of Bunthorne's stage performance, adjusted to fit Kettle.

When I go out of door
Of Suffragettes a score
All pleading and screaming
Of " Votes for Women '
Will follow me as before.

I'shall, in cultured speech,
Endorse the views of each:
That fair agitators
Shall be legislators—
Whene'er Home Rule we reach.

A pushful, pale young man,
A lady M.P.'s young man,
An ultra—statistical
Quite—optimistical
Five-o'clock-tea young man.

Conceive me if you can,
A *Nationist* young man ;
A keep-your-hat-on
Till-the-Anthem-is-done,
With a lock-up-the-organ plan.

Whose gospel ".Out-and-out,"
You daily hear him shout,
Till to Parliament sent he
Sings " *festina lente* "
In a pianissimo spout.

A wide-awake young man,
A *Place aux dames* ! young man
Politic economist,
Irish autonomist,
Sing-on-the-hob young man.

The parliamentary Bunthorne.

April 1910, p. 217

Militant suffragettes conducted a campaign of arson in 1912 to draw public attention to their cause. Pillar-boxes were targeted in cities across Britain and thousands of letters were destroyed. SPEX takes a light-hearted look at one proposed solution, to have the army operate a military postal system with the public sorting their letters in advance. A line of soldiers, each with an appropriate expression, collects demands for payment, polite evasions and charitable donations etc. One fashionably dressed young woman receives a flirtatious salute from the soldier responsible for love letters. The suffragettes' arson campaign did not reach Dublin but SPEX, who may have worked from London, and the Irish public in general were well aware of it.

FROM PILLAR TO POST.

Finding that they cannot protect the ordinary pillar-boxes in the streets from the fury of the Militant Suffragettes, the authorities seriously contemplate establishing a Military Post, each Tommy to represent a post-box, and leave the rest to him—and fate.

From pillar to post.
March 1912, p. 299

Newspapers were filled with reports of attacks on property, arrests and hunger strikes as the suffragettes' campaign of militant action expanded into 1912. To conservative minds it must all have been most distressing - so perhaps SPEX is poking fun at alarmist predictions of the fall of civilisation. A hatchet-wielding French revolutionary, wearing her Liberty Cap and sword, inspires her modern-day sister-in-arms to follow her lead and 'Smash Everything'. Destruction follows in their wake as they trample on law and order.

History repeating herself.
March 1912, p. 291

Only a few years before the introduction of female police on Dublin's streets the very idea seemed preposterous to SHY – and perhaps to many of his readers. According to the caption New York was considering such a move, but this three-frame cartoon neatly illustrates the lack of authority which women held in society. Tipsy young men approach a demure 'constable-ess' to walk them home, a fashion-conscious officer wears her helmet at a jaunty angle and even fishwives would not respect a policewoman. However, The *Lepracaun*'s American information was incomplete; while it did not have a separate corps of policewomen, by 1903 New York had women on the force and in 1912 it appointed its first female detective.

A new force.
March 1913, p. 127

This alarming suffragette, with her wild hair and mad eyes, firmly grips a hammer - the tool of her trade. Her bomb and paraffin sit ready for action as the city skyline blazes away behind her. Significantly, SPEX shows her leaning on the ballot box with a caption asking 'When..? (not 'If'), conceding that women will eventually gain the vote. The militants' campaign of destruction cost them much public sympathy and made some worry what sort of voters such women would become.

When she gets it, what will she do with it?

When she gets it, what will she do with it?
May 1913, p. 151

After years of peaceful suffragist lobbying and violent suffragette action it is somewhat shocking to see this cartoon by SHY appearing as late as 1914. As explained in the caption, blonde women are more troublesome. The cartoonist's jocular remedy is to pitch a bucket of tar over the offending female, which will also (apparently) elicit her immediate apology. Intended as a joke, the cartoon does reflect the tradition of pouring tar and feathers over people (frequently women) who stepped outside their socially approved roles. In fairness to SHY, the husband is not drawn as the most attractive, upright or noble of characters.

A Judge of the Supreme Court, New York, has given as his opinion that blonde women figure more in cases of domestic trouble than do their darker sisters. Now we wonder was that Judge judging fairly, and if such be the case would it be a good idea to lessen fair-headed people's tendencies to trouble by dyeing their hair a dark shade? We commend the accompanying pictures as a suggestion to young men who worry over their fair charmer's spasms of scrapping moods.

January 1914, p. 260

Labour

In August 1911 Dublin newsboys went on strike for better pay, blocking newspaper offices, overturning their delivery vans and destroying bundles of papers. Serious street violence broke out as police and strikers exchanged blows and baton-charges met a hail of stone. Observers noted that 'respectably-dressed people and shop assistants' joined the fray, along with 'tailors, labourers, tram workers, youths and women'.[128] Here SPEX shows an enraged Dublin Metropolitan Policeman on O'Connell Street (then Sackville Street) beating a crowd of women and children into submission, with a forest of raised police batons doing likewise in the background. On top of his pillar Admiral Nelson joins in the mêlée by dancing a hornpipe. The policeman's rural origins are evident from his accent in the caption "Sthrike, Indade!", where he refers to a 1907 strike by police in Belfast – when the authorities did not see fit to launch a baton charge against the strikers. (see also 'The Real Strikers' page 193)

---

128 *Irish Times*, 26 Aug. 1911, p.1.

STRIKE! — BUT NOT HERE.

BOBBY: "Sthrike, indade! The idaya! D'yez think yiz are Polismen an' can sthrike whin an' who yez like? :But I'll show yez the differ between or'nary citizens an' pace officers." (Whack—whack—whack !)

Strike! - but not here.
September 1911, p. 223

A strike on the railways in September 1911 led to many workers being laid off as winter approaches, with terrible consequences for their families. SPEX's opinion of the trade union leadership is made clear in this cartoon from November 1911. The workers' representatives sit in a pub dining on hearty stew and fine champagne while the dejected worker and his hungry family sit by an empty grate beneath hollow slogans. The caption is from the *Irish Daily Independent*, the newspaper owned by William Martin Murphy who would go on to lead Dublin's employers in the Lockout of 1913. (See also 'Sports for March', page 191)

AFTER THE BATTLE.

From *The Irish Daily Independent*—"The people in the back streets of Dublin, the lecturer said, never knew a winter, nor for that matter a summer, in which they had enough to eat. This winter they would be a little nearer the starvation line than usual, for the harvest of the recent strikes had not yet been fully reaped, and the children would feel the pinch first."

After the battle.
November 1911, p. 243

A satirical German Kaiser and British 'Jack Tar' play battleships. Rivalry between the British and German imperial fleets led to huge sums being invested in new and ever larger battleships in the years before the Great War. This was also an important period for the development of international socialism. The SPEX cartoon shows how workers from Germany and Britain understood that, regardless of who won the arms race, it was the ordinary worker that would end up paying the price in increased taxes and reduced spending on basic welfare. Given the magazine's occasionally hostile attitude to labour politics it is interesting to see SPEX propose united action by the working class in both countries to curb this deadly imperial competition.

The war confidence trick; or beggar my neighbour.
June 1912, p. 23

In an anti-strike cartoon from March 1913 SHY shows a Dublin worker being led astray by a mad March hare labelled 'Strikes'. Plunging into debt and heading for poverty and starvation, the duped worker is leaving 'employment and industry', the factory and docks, far behind. The belief that the trade union leadership were misleading the ordinary workers into a costly strike appears in other *Lepracaun* cartoons of the period. (See also 'After the Battle', page 187)

Sports for March – following the Mad Hare.
March 1913, p. 135

During the General Strike and Lockout of 1913 the police launched a baton charge against a crowd gathered on O'Connell Street (Sackville Street) to hear a speech by the union leader Jim Larkin. The street was busy with people out for a Sunday stroll and many Dubliners unconnected with the Lockout were caught up in the violence. Public opinion was scandalised at the uncontrolled ferocity of the police action, so SPEX presents us with his famous image of a maniacal policeman, helmet askew and truncheon raised, holding an injured infant like a rag doll as a respectably dressed woman (perhaps the child's mother) lies unconscious at his feet. *The Lepracaun Cartoon Monthly* did not support Larkin or the trade union movement, but this full-page cartoon is a clear condemnation of the official over-reaction. (See also Strike! - but not here, page 185)

THE REAL STRIKERS

On August 30 and 31 the Dublin Metropolitan Police and the R. I. Constabulary ran "amok" in the City of Dublin. Result: Two men batoned to death and several hundred men, women and children badly beaten, whose ages range from one week to ninety years.

The real strikers.
October 1913, p. 215

These two cartoons satirise the spreading effect of the General Strike and Lockout of 1913, they also give us a glimpse of middle-class babyhood at the time. The wicker cradle and frilly bonnets are not so strange, but feeding-bottles made of ordinary glass seem alarming today. The babies in the first cartoon refuse to use non-union goods while the second image shows the social boycott of anyone connected with strike-breakers. 'Scab' was a loud and serious cry in 1913.

Strikes the fashion.

October 1913, p. 220

In this SPEX cartoon from October 1913, at the height of the Lockout, the employers and trade unions are shown as being equally to blame. Poised for the attack, the employer with his 'lock out' sword and the worker with his 'strike' club have brought industry in the city to a standstill. The tools of their trades, the accounts book and hammer, lie abandoned at their feet. In the background tens of thousands of unemployed can be seen crowding into the workhouse.

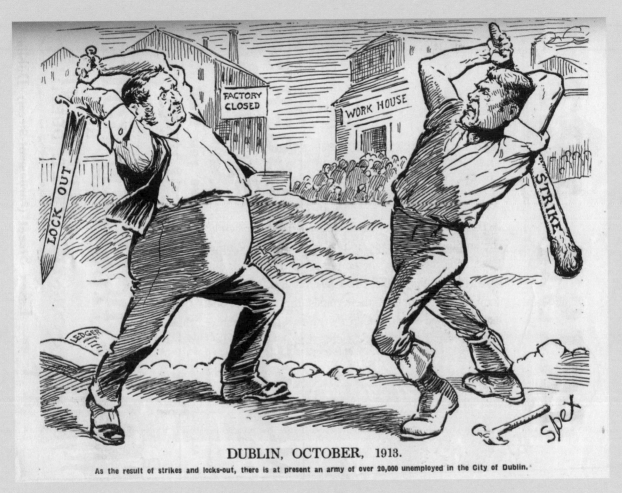

DUBLIN, OCTOBER, 1913.

As the result of strikes and locks-out, there is at present an army of over 20,000 unemployed in the City of Dublin.

Dublin, October 1913.
October 1913, p. 211

A month later, in November 1913, SPEX shows the worker and employer coming to blows. In their mutual hatred they trample on the general public – the real victim of the dispute according to the Lepracaun. From a safe distance he warns them that the city and its people cannot take much more of this bitter dispute. The workhouse is full up so the poor of the city have nowhere to turn for relief. After months of deadlock the protagonists are no longer presented as individuals but as the opposing causes of 'Labour' and 'Capital', suggesting that readers understood the larger political and economic forces behind the confrontation.[129]

---

129 For a digital gallery of *Lepracaun* cartons relating to the 1913 Lockout, compiled by James Curry, see: http://dublincitypubliclibraries.com/image-galleries/treasures-collections/lepracaun-cartoon-monthly-and-1913-14-dublin-lockout

FLATTENING HIM OUT.

Mr. LEPRACAUN: " Gentlemen, our friend on the ground appears to be getting the worst of it, and as he has to pay for the music you might stop before he is past repairing."

[The Labour deadlock in Dublin, which has now lasted over two months, has been a greater disaster to the general public than to the parties engaged in the conflict.]

Flattening him out.
November 1913, p. 223